Chess Tactics
Workbook for Kids

John Nunn

TRAPPED PIECE

GAMBIT

First published in the UK by Gambit Publications Ltd 2019

ISBN-13: 978-1-911465-31-7
ISBN-10: 1-911465-31-7

DISTRIBUTION:
Worldwide (except USA): Central Books Ltd, 50 Freshwater Road, Chadwell Heath, London RM8 1RX, England. Tel +44 (0)20 8986 4854 Fax +44 (0)20 8533 5821.
E-mail: orders@Centralbooks.com

Gambit Publications Ltd, 50 Freshwater Road, Chadwell Heath, London RM8 1RX, England.
E-mail: info@gambitbooks.com
Website (regularly updated): www.gambitbooks.com

Edited by Graham Burgess
Typeset by John Nunn
All illustrations by Shane Mercer
Printed in the USA by Bang Printing, Brainerd, Minnesota

10 9 8 7 6 5 4 3 2 1

Gambit Publications Ltd
Directors: Dr John Nunn GM, Murray Chandler GM, and Graham Burgess FM
German Editor: Petra Nunn WFM

Contents

Chess Notation

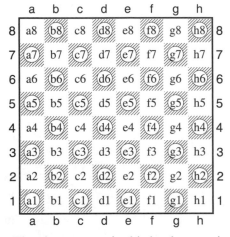

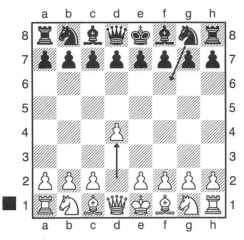

The chess moves in this book are written in the standard chess *notation* that is in use throughout the world. It can be learned by anyone in just a few minutes.

As you can see from the left-hand chessboard above, the vertical columns of squares (called *files*) are labelled a-h and the horizontal rows of squares (called *ranks*) are numbered 1-8. This gives each square a unique name. The pieces are shown as follows:

Knight = ♞
Bishop = ♝
Rook = ♜
Queen = ♛
King = ♚

Pawns are not given a symbol. When they move, only the *destination square* is given.

In the right-hand diagram above, White has already played the move **1 d4**. The **1** indicates the move-number, and **d4** the destination square of the white pawn. Black is about to reply **1...♞f6** (moving his knight to the **f6-square** on his *first move*).

The following additional symbols are also used:

Check	=	+
Double check	=	++
Capture	=	x
Checkmate	=	#
Castles kingside	=	0-0
Castles queenside	=	0-0-0
Good move	=	!
Bad move	=	?
Brilliant move	=	!!
Disastrous move	=	??

To check you've got the hang of it, play through the following moves on your chessboard: **1 e4 e6 2 d4 d5 3 ♞c3 ♞f6 4 e5 ♞fd7** (both knights can move to d7, so this notation shows that it is the knight on the f-file that moves to d7) **5 f4 c5 6 ♞f3 ♞c6 7 ♝e3 a6 8 ♝e2 ♛b6 9 a3 cxd4** (this means that the pawn on the c-file captures on d4) **10 ♞xd4 ♛xb2??** (not a good move). You should now have reached the position shown in Exercise 1 of Chapter 9 (page 83).

Introduction

The famous chess-player Richard Teichmann once said that chess is 99% tactics. There is no doubt that most games are decided by *tactics*, while we'll define as "forcing sequences of moves aiming to either mate or secure a material advantage". The goal of this book is to provide a grounding in all the main types of chess tactics. Each tactical idea is introduced with a brief explanation, followed by a set of exercises. Within each chapter, the exercises gradually increase in difficulty. As some exercises build on earlier ones, it is best if they are tackled in sequence. Each chapter ends with a page of exercises in which you have to *counter* the tactic you are studying. The positions have almost all been chosen to feature ideas that occur regularly in games, although I have added a few amazing positions more for fun.

Don't be discouraged if you have problems solving some of the exercises, especially towards the end of the chapters. Once you have made a serious effort to solve a position, read the solution and learn everything you can from it. Then the next time you see the position or a similar one, you will find the key idea more easily. Learning tactics is the main aim of this book, and finding them over the board will be the ultimate reward for your hard work reading it.

This book is aimed at readers who know the rules of chess and want to start winning games. Learning tactics is the best way to improve your chess quickly. *Strategy*, that is to say long-term planning, becomes important at a more advanced level, but even excellent strategy won't help you unless you have a good grasp of tactics.

In each exercise, the aim is either to mate or to gain material. If you can't give mate, winning material is the next best thing. To check whether you are winning material, use the standard table of material values:

Queen	=	9 points	Bishop	=	3 points
Rook	=	5 points	Knight	=	3 points
	Pawn	=	1 point		

Thus winning a queen for a rook and a knight gains 9 points in return for 8, a net gain of 1 point. Winning a bishop and a knight for a rook is also a gain of 1 point.

A small white or black square next to the diagram shows which player is to move and this is usually also stated under the diagram. In most exercises you should start at the diagram position and try to find the best move, but in a few cases you are asked to find the best reply to a particular move by the opponent. The exercises have been carefully chosen so that there is one clearly best solution and they have all been computer-checked for correctness. Each chapter ends with a set of solutions, which often contain additional instructive comments.

While each chapter focuses on a particular theme, it's important to recognize that tactical ideas often work best in combination with one another. So don't divide up tactics into separate compartments, and keep thinking flexibly. The book ends with a series of test papers (with points awarded for the correct answers) featuring a mix of tactical ideas. Good luck!

John Nunn

1 Fork

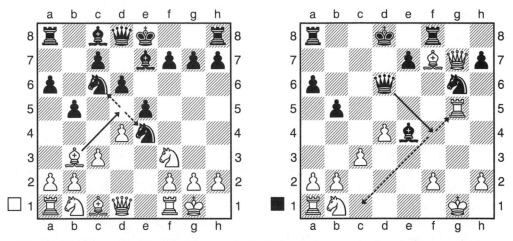

The *fork* is the most common chess tactic. In its basic form, one of your pieces attacks two enemy pieces at the same time. The left-hand diagram above is a good example. The two black knights are both undefended and lie on the same diagonal. White plays **1 ♗d5**, attacking the two knights. It's impossible for Black to defend both at the same time, so one knight is lost. Undefended pieces, such as the knights here, are often vulnerable to forks. A fork that gives a check is especially effective, because a check demands an immediate response.

It's not always the case that a fork involves an attack on two enemy pieces. It can be, for example, that one 'prong' of the fork targets a piece, while another creates a threat of mate. The concept is still the same, that of one piece making two threats which cannot both be met, but this more refined version can be harder to spot. The right-hand diagram above is a case in point. Black plays **1...♕f4**, threatening both 2...♕c1# and 2...♕xg5+. White cannot counter both the mate threat and the attack on the undefended rook. The queen and knight are the best pieces for delivering forks, as both have the power to operate in eight different directions, but any piece is capable of giving a fork.

Here are some tips for solving the exercises:
- Look for undefended enemy pieces, as they may be vulnerable to forks. On the other hand, if you have undefended pieces, take care not to allow your opponent to fork them.
- Every check is a potential fork.
- In most of the exercises, the fork has to be set up by a preliminary action. This is generally a forcing move of some sort, such as a check or capture.

Exercises

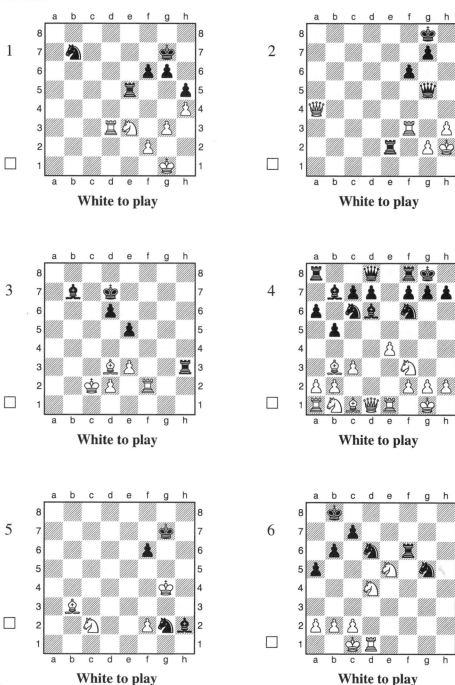

1 White to play

2 White to play

3 White to play

4 White to play

5 White to play

6 White to play

7

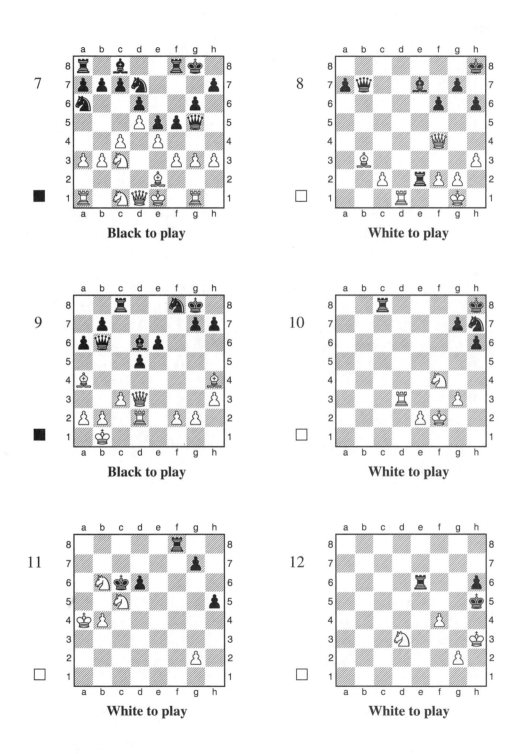

7 Black to play

8 White to play

9 Black to play

10 White to play

11 White to play

12 White to play

13

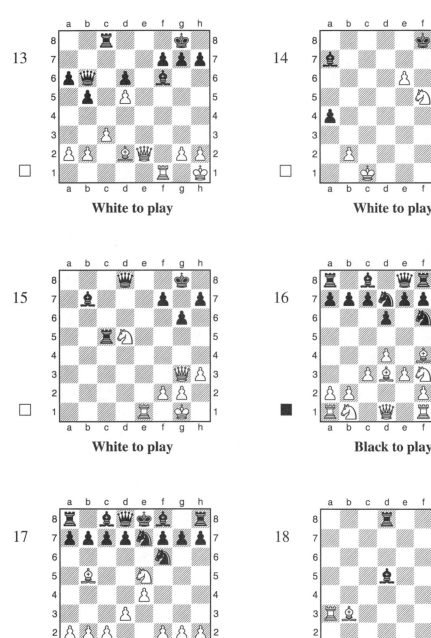

White to play

14

White to play

15

White to play

16

Black to play

17

Black to play

18

White to play

19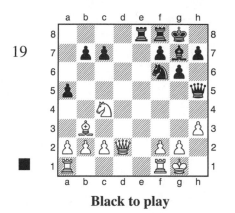

Black to play

20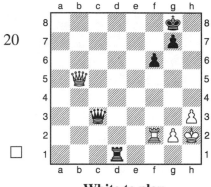

White to play

21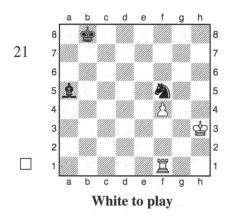

White to play

22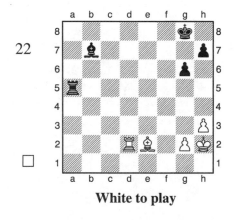

White to play

23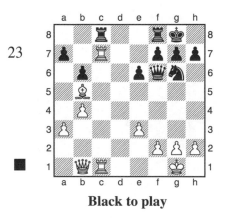

Black to play

24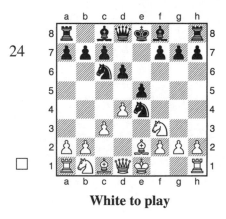

White to play

10

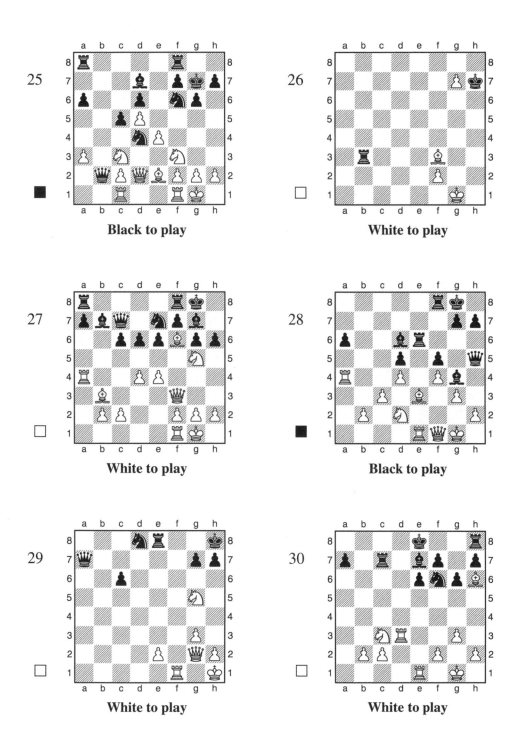

25   **Black to play**

26   **White to play**

27   **White to play**

28   **Black to play**

29   **White to play**

30   **White to play**

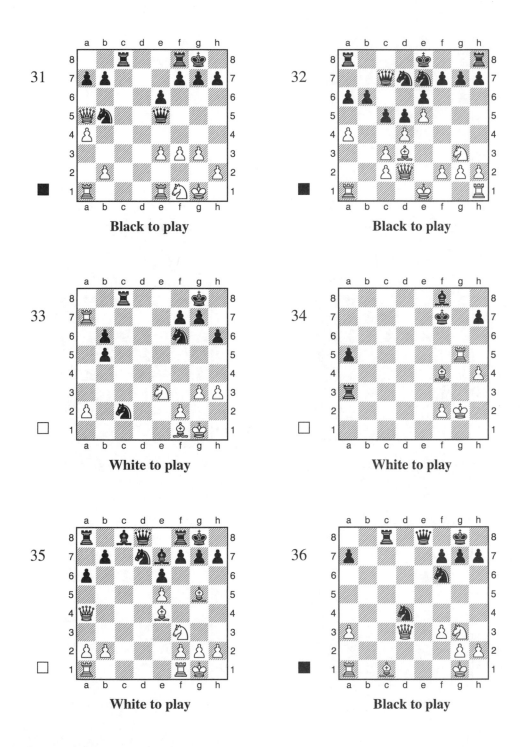

31   **Black to play**

32   **Black to play**

33   **White to play**

34   **White to play**

35   **White to play**

36   **Black to play**

37

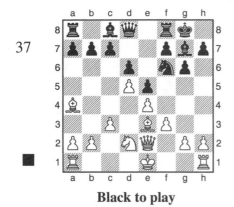

Black to play

38

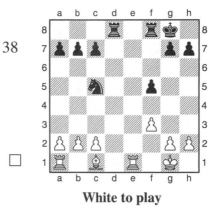

White to play

39

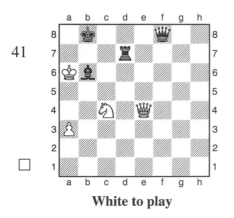

Black to play

40

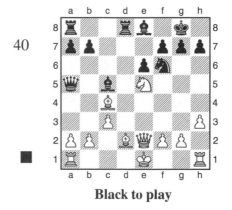

Black to play

41

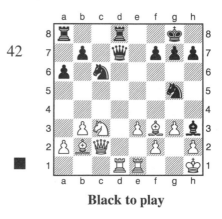

White to play

42

Black to play

43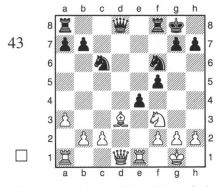

White's bishop and knight are forked. Is there any escape?

44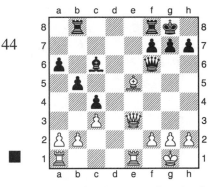

How should Black respond to the fork of queen and rook?

45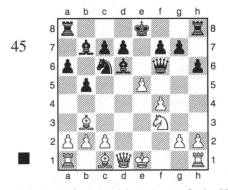

Black is faced with a pawn fork. How should he continue?

46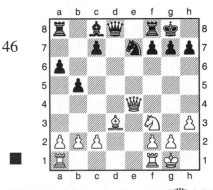

White has the twin threats of ♕xh7# and ♕xa8. What is Black's best response?

47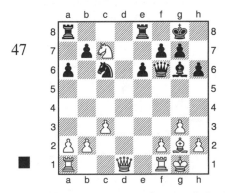

Both black rooks are under attack. Is there an escape route?

48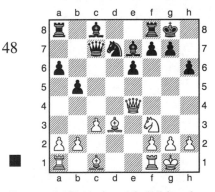

Just as in Exercise 46, White threatens ♕h7#, but this time the solution is completely different. Can you find it?

Solutions to Fork Exercises

1) 1 ♖d7+ is a typical fork. White checks the black king and attacks the b7-knight. After the king moves, White simply takes the knight and wins a piece.

2) White has several checks, for example on b3, c4 and a8, but only one wins Black's rook: **1 ♕c4+**.

3) 1 ♗f5+ is a diagonal fork winning Black's rook.

4) 1 e5 forks bishop and knight and so wins a piece. The pawn must be sufficiently defended for this type of idea to work. Here it is attacked twice and defended twice, so Black also loses a piece if he takes the pawn.

5) Even the king is capable of delivering a fork: **1 ♔h3** attacks bishop and knight, winning a piece and the game.

6) White has three different knight checks, two harmless but one winning the black rook: **1 ♘d7+**.

7) The undefended c3-knight and g1-rook are vulnerable to the queen fork **1...♕e3**, when Black wins.

8) This is an example of a fork which targets an enemy piece and a mate threat rather than two enemy pieces. The deadly **1 ♕c4** sets up the twin threats of 2 ♕xe2 and 2 ♕g8#, and so wins the rook.

9) You should have spotted the undefended bishops on a4 and h4, a sign that a fork is in the air. Black can exploit them by **1...♖c4**, winning a piece.

10) A preliminary check drives the black king into position for a fork: **1 ♘g6+ ♔g8 2 ♘e7+** and White wins the black rook.

11) Two knights working together can produce an amazing array of forks. After **1 b5+** there's no escape: **1...♔xb6 2 ♘d7+**, **1...♔c7 2 ♘e6+** or **1...♔xc5 2 ♘d7+** and Black loses his rook in every case.

12) **1 g4+ ♔g6 2 f5+** wins the rook.

13) A preliminary sacrifice opens the g-file and leads to a fork of king and rook: **1 ♖xf6! gxf6 2 ♕g4+** followed by **♕xc8+**.

14) Knights are very good at delivering forks and are a danger even in the endgame: **1 e7+ ♔e8 2 ♘d6+ ♔xe7** (or else the pawn promotes) **3 ♘c8+** and White wins the bishop.

15) A *decoy* (see Chapter 4) draws the black queen to a square allowing a fork: **1 ♖e8+! ♕xe8 2 ♘f6+ ♔f8 3 ♘xe8** and White wins queen for rook because **3...♔xe8** loses the rook to a second fork after **4 ♕e3+**.

16) Black can exploit the bunched-up white pieces in the centre by **1...e5 2 dxe5 dxe5 3 ♗g5** (or any other square) **3...e4**, winning a piece.

17) The undefended e5-knight is the victim here: **1...c6** attacks the bishop and after **2 ♗c4** (2 ♗a4 is the same) **2...♕a5+** Black wins a piece.

18) In a surprising twist, White invests a rook to win rook and bishop: **1 ♖a8! ♖xa8** (1...♗xb3 2 ♖xd8+ also wins for White) **2 ♗xd5+** followed by **3 ♗xa8**, and White is a piece up.

19) Black's pawns are the heroes here. One pawn sacrifices itself by **1...a4!** to allow another to fork two pieces after **2 ♗xa4 b5**.

20) A 'billiard ball' manoeuvre by the white queen wins a rook: **1 ♕e8+ ♔h7 2 ♕h5+ ♔g8 3 ♕xd1**.

21) **1 ♖b1+ ♔c7** (or any other square) **2 ♖b5** and White wins a piece.

22) A preliminary check drives Black's king into position for a decisive fork: **1 ♖d8+ ♔f7 2 ♖d7+**, winning the bishop.

23) Black first swaps rooks and then forks rook and bishop: **1...♖xc7 2 ♖xc7 ♕e5**.

24) After driving one knight away, White wins the other with a queen fork: **1 d5 ♘e7** (or any other square) **2 ♕a4+**.

25) A typical queen offer is followed by a knight fork: **1...♕xc3! 2 ♕xc3 ♘xe2+** and Black wins two pieces.

26) **1 g8♕+!** (not 1 ♗d5? ♖b1+ followed by 2...♔xg7, and Black escapes) **1...♔xg8 2 ♗d5+** wins the rook and the game.

27) A surprise queen sacrifice wins at least two pawns: **1 ♗xg7 ♔xg7 2 ♕xf7+! ♖xf7 3 ♘xe6+** and **4 ♘xc7**.

28) Retreating moves are generally harder to spot than ones that advance. Here **1...♕e8!** pulls the queen back, but wins a piece by attacking both a4 and e3.

29) White has the knock-out blow **1 ♕e4!**, threatening both 2 ♕xe8# and 2 ♕xh7#. If **1...♖xe4**, then **2 ♖f8#**.

30) Two forks in a row prove too much for Black: **1 ♗g7** (forking rook and knight) **1...♖g8 2 ♗xf6 ♗xf6 3 ♘d5** and now it is the other rook and the bishop which are forked. Note that the e6-pawn is *pinned* against the black king (see Chapter 2) and so cannot take the knight.

31) The b5-knight is *pinned* against the black queen and appears lost, but by a neat trick Black not only saves the knight, but also wins a pawn: **1...♘d4! 2 ♕xe5 ♘xf3+** followed by **3...♘xe5**.

32) There's no immediate fork, but a preliminary pawn exchange sets one up: **1...cxd4 2 cxd4 ♘xe5! 3 dxe5** (or else Black simply wins a pawn) **3...♕xe5+** and the rook on a1 falls.

33) It's often necessary to plan ahead. Here two preliminary moves create the conditions for a bishop fork: **1 ♘xc2 ♖xc2 2 ♖a8+ ♔h7 3 ♗d3+** and White wins the rook.

34) The fork is well-concealed here and requires some preparation: **1 ♖f5+ ♔g8** (any other king move is also met by taking on f8) **2 ♖xf8+! ♔xf8 3 ♗d6+** and White ends up a piece ahead.

35) A preliminary bishop sacrifice is necessary: **1 ♗xh7+! ♔xh7 2 ♕h4+** (first fork: king and e7-bishop) **2...♔g8 3 ♕xe7** and the second fork of queen and f8-rook leaves White rook and pawn for bishop ahead.

36) A queen swap sets up a lethal fork: **1...♕e1+ 2 ♕f1** (2 ♘f1 ♘e2+ also wins for Black) **2...♕xf1+ 3 ♔xf1 ♘b3** forks rook and bishop, and wins a piece.

37) Undefended pieces are always vulnerable to forks. Here the a4-bishop hardly looks in danger, but with two precise moves Black wins an important pawn: **1...♘xd5! 2 exd5 ♕h4+** followed by **3...♕xa4**.

38) This 19th-century trap has caught a number of victims: **1 ♗g5** (when the d8-rook moves, White intends ♗e7, forking rook and knight) **1...♖d5** (Black counters by defending the knight in advance, but it doesn't save the game) **2 ♗e7** (White must play his moves in the right order: swapping them round doesn't work because 2 c4? ♖d7 3 ♗e7 can be met by 3...♘d3!) **2...♖e8 3 c4** and now the d5-rook must move away, whereupon the knight falls.

39) Black strikes with **1...♗e2! 2 ♖xe2** (forced, as the queen has no move) **2...♖c1!** and after **3 ♖e1** (3 ♕xc1 ♘xe2+ is even worse) **3...♖xd1 4 ♖xd1** he has won queen for rook and bishop.

40) Black wins material with the surprising **1...♗xf2+! 2 ♔xf2** (2 ♕xf2 is relatively best, but can be answered by either 2...♘e4 or 2...♕xe5+ with at least an extra pawn for Black) **2...♖xd2! 3 ♕xd2 ♘e4+** and the white queen is lost.

41) Here's a spot of fun. A queen sacrifice leads to a cascade of knight forks: **1 ♕a8+!! ♔xa8 2 ♘xb6+ ♔b8 3 ♘xd7+** followed by **4 ♘xf8**, and White wins.

42) Black's queen is under attack, but he can ignore this and play for a knight fork: **1...♘xf3! 2 ♖xd7 ♗g2+!** (a beautiful idea, enabling the f3-knight to wreak havoc in White's position) **3 ♔xg2 ♘xe1+ 4 ♔f1 ♘xc2** and Black has won a rook.

43) After **1 ♗c4+** the bishop escapes from attack with check. Black has to deal with the check, giving White time to save the knight as well. After **1...♔h8 2 ♕xd8 ♖axd8 3 ♘g5** the position is level.

44) **1...♕g6** is the only way to save both pieces. White must meet the threat of 2...♕xg2#, and then Black can move the attacked rook.

45) **1...♕e7** is the right choice, *pinning* the e5-pawn against the white king. After **2 0-0 ♗c5+ 3 ♔h1 0-0-0**, for example, the position is level. Note that 1...♗b4+? is wrong because after 2 c3 Black really does lose a piece.

46) **1...♗f5** is the only move to solve Black's problem. He directly blocks the route from e4 to h7, and by clearing the back rank allows the queen to defend the rook on a8.

47) **1...♖ed8** is the way out, attacking the white queen and so gaining time to rescue the other rook. Then **2 ♘xa8 ♖xd1 3 ♖axd1 ♗h5** is good for Black, as White's knight is seriously out of play on a8. Note that the apparently similar 1...♖ad8? is bad, as 2 ♘xe8 attacks Black's queen and wins material.

48) Black can avoid material loss by **1...♘f6!** (1...g6? 2 ♗xh6 and 1...f5? 2 ♕xe6+ both lose a pawn). Then **2 ♕xa8** (the rook has gone, but the queen gets trapped in the corner) **2...♗b7 3 ♗f4** (after 3 ♕a7? ♗c5 4 ♗f4 ♕c6 the queen is lost, giving Black the advantage) **3...♕c6 4 ♕xf8+ ♗xf8** is relatively best, but still fine for Black since his active pieces compensate for his slight material disadvantage.

FORK

17

2 Pin

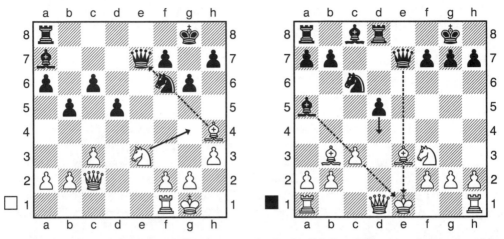

It's easiest to explain the *pin* with an example. In the left-hand diagram above, the white bishop lies on the same diagonal as Black's knight and queen. If the knight moves, the bishop can take the queen. Since the queen is so valuable, the knight is effectively immobilized and cannot move. White is not threatening to take the knight at once, since ♗xf6 can be met by the recapture ...♕xf6, but if the knight is attacked again, Black will be in serious trouble. White can achieve this by **1 ♘g4**, when Black loses a piece since he cannot defend the knight a second time (1...♔g7 2 ♗xf6+ costs him his queen). A pinned piece is generally paralysed (although there are exceptions – see Exercise 41) and if it is repeatedly attacked then it is likely to be lost. Given time, pinned pieces can generally be unpinned. For example, if it were Black to move in the diagram then 1...♕e6 would relieve the pin. It follows that pins have to be exploited quickly, or the chance may be gone.

The general arrangement of a pin is that one of your line-moving pieces (that is, queen, rook or bishop) lies on the same line as two enemy pieces. The *front* enemy piece is the one that is pinned. If it moves, you can take the *rear* piece. The more valuable the rear piece, the more effective the pin. If the rear piece is the king, then moving the front piece would even be an illegal move. In the right-hand diagram above, there are two pins against the white king. The e3-bishop is pinned by the black queen, while the c3-pawn is pinned by the bishop on a5. Black wins a piece by **1...d4**, attacking the immobilized bishop on e3. Neither the bishop nor the pawn can take on d4, as both are pinned, while **2 ♘xd4 ♘xd4** (or 2...♖xd4) costs White a piece, as does leaving the bishop to be taken next move.

Here are some tips for solving the exercises:

• A piece which is apparently defended by a pinned piece may not be defended at all (see Exercise 1, for example).

• Can you make a preliminary exchange or sacrifice to draw a piece into position for a pin?

• The combination of pin and fork is often deadly (see Exercise 6 for one example).

18

Exercises

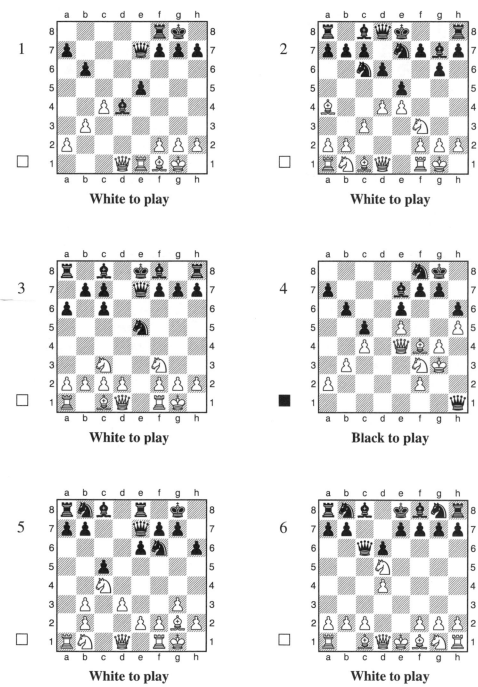

1 — White to play

2 — White to play

3 — White to play

4 — Black to play

5 — White to play

6 — White to play

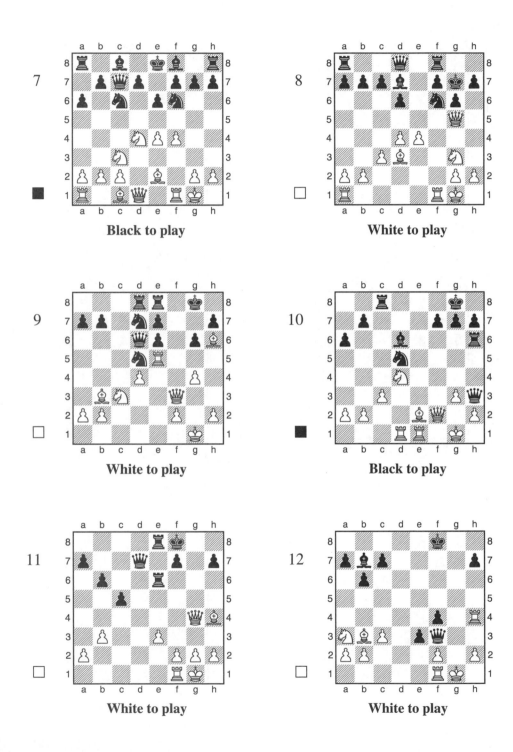

7 Black to play

8 White to play

9 White to play

10 Black to play

11 White to play

12 White to play

20

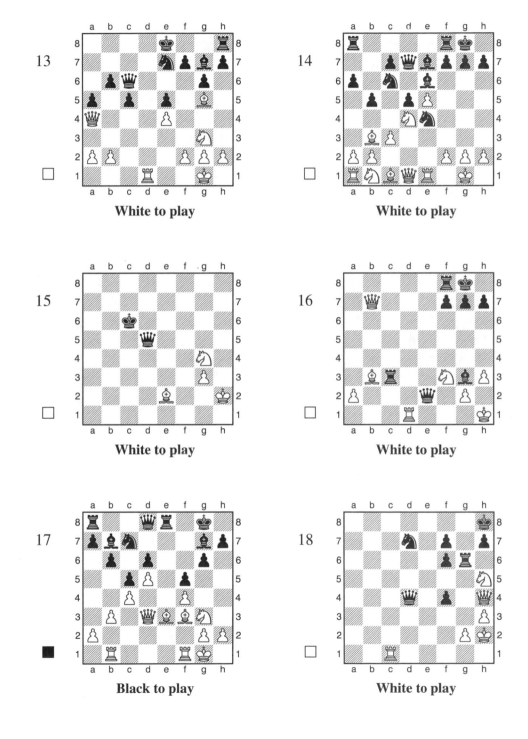

13   **White to play**

14   **White to play**

15   **White to play**

16   **White to play**

17   **Black to play**

18   **White to play**

19

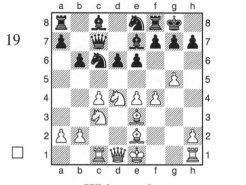

White to play

20

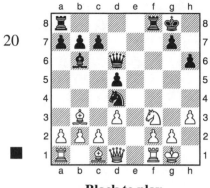

Black to play

21

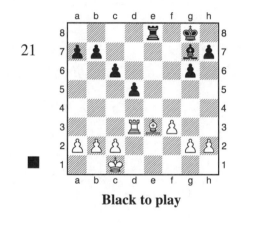

Black to play

22

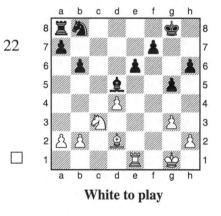

White to play

23

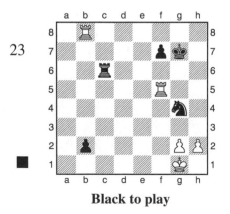

Black to play

24

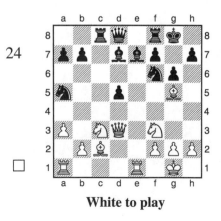

White to play

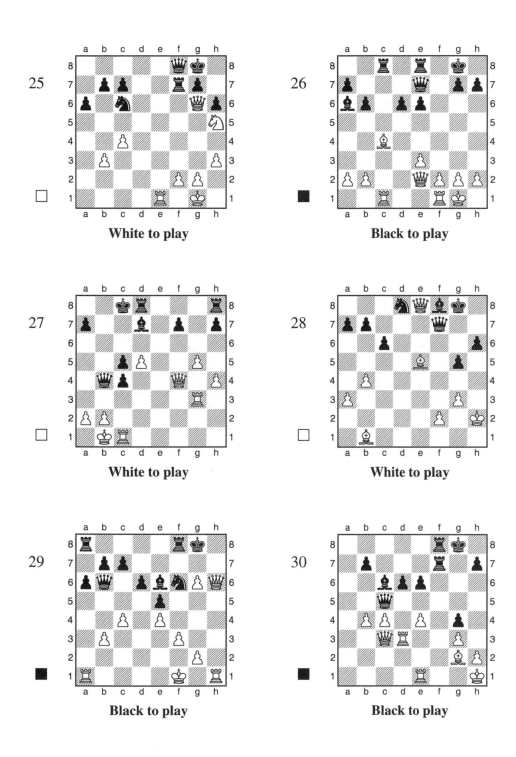

25 White to play

26 Black to play

27 White to play

28 White to play

29 Black to play

30 Black to play

31
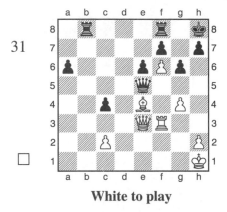
White to play

32
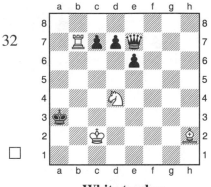
White to play

33
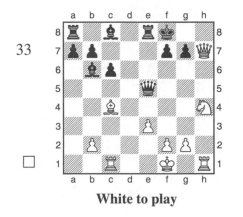
White to play

34
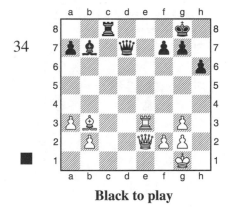
Black to play

35
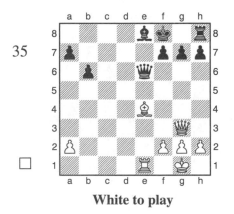
White to play

36
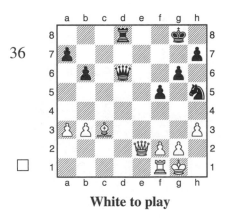
White to play

Does the Tactic Work?

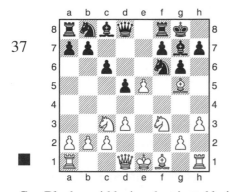

37

Can Black avoid losing the pinned knight on f6?

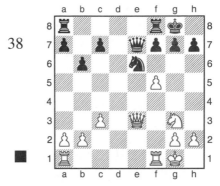

38

Is the pinned e6-knight doomed?

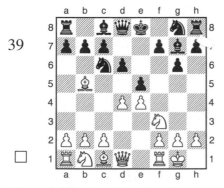

39

Does **1 d5** win a piece here?

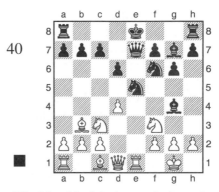

40

Black's e5-knight is caught in a pin. Is it doomed?

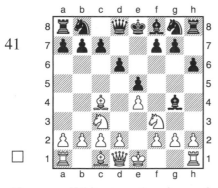

41

How can White turn the pin on the f3-knight to his advantage?

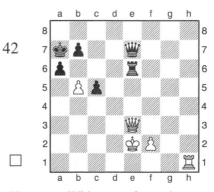

42

How can White transform the apparent loss of his queen into a win?

Solutions to Pin Exercises

1) The pin along the e-file means that the bishop isn't really defended by the e5-pawn, so **1 ♕xd4! exd4 2 ♖xe7** wins a piece.

2) If you cannot take a pinned piece at once, look for a way to attack it again. Here **1 d5** wins the pinned knight on c6 for a pawn.

3) **1 ♘xe5** (1 ♖e1? ♘xf3+ 2 gxf3 ♗e6 lets Black escape) **1...♕xe5 2 ♖e1** pins and wins the queen.

4) The f3-knight is pinned, so **1...♗h4+!** wins since the queen is lost after **2 ♘xh4 ♕xe4**.

5) The pin on the a7-pawn allows White to win rook for knight by **1 ♘b6! axb6 2 ♖xa8**.

6) White wins with a pin-fork combination that sometimes occurs in the opening part of the game: **1 ♗b5! ♕xb5 2 ♘c7+** and the queen is lost.

7) White has just played f4, opening up the diagonal leading to his king. Black exploited this blunder to win by **1...♘xd4 2 ♕xd4 ♗c5**, pinning the queen.

8) The g6-pawn is pinned, so **1 ♖xf6! ♕xf6 2 ♘h5+** wins by forking king and queen.

9) **1 ♖xe6!** breaks open the diagonal from b3 to g8 and after **1...♕xe6 2 ♗xd5** White wins the queen. Not, however, 1 ♘xd5? ♘xe5 2 dxe5 ♕c6!, when Black wins.

10) **1...♗xg3! 2 ♕xg3** (or 2 hxg3 ♕h1#) **2...♖g6** wins the white queen with a pin.

11) **1 ♗f6** threatens 2 ♕g7# and exploits the pin on the e6-rook. Then **1...♖xf6** (or 1...♖c8 2 ♕g7+ ♔e8 3 ♕g8#) **2 ♕xd7** gives White a decisive material advantage.

12) White is threatened with immediate mate, but can turn the tables by **1 ♖xf4+! ♕xf4 2 fxe3**, winning the queen and emerging a piece up.

13) **1 ♖d8+!** draws the enemy king into a pin, so after **1...♔xd8 2 ♕xc6** Black cannot recapture.

14) White can win a piece by **1 ♘xe6 fxe6** (1...♕xe6 also loses to 2 ♖xe4) **2 ♖xe4** since the d-pawn is pinned against the undefended queen.

15) The pin-fork combination punch wins Black's queen by **1 ♗f3! ♕xf3 2 ♘e5+**.

16) White breaks through with **1 ♕xf7+! ♖xf7 2 ♖d8+ ♕e8** (the black rook on f7 cannot interpose as it is pinned) **3 ♖xe8#**.

17) A small sacrifice sets up a deadly pin after **1...♖xe3! 2 ♕xe3 ♗d4**, winning the queen.

18) Black's exposed king is his downfall: **1 ♖c8+ ♖g8 2 ♕g4!** and the black rook is pinned, so there is no defence against the triple threat of 3 ♕g7#, 3 ♕xg8# and 3 ♖xg8#.

19) White exploits the line-up of c1-rook and black queen on c7 by **1 ♘d5! exd5** (1...♕d7 2 ♘xc6 also wins material) **2 cxd5** and the c6-knight is pinned and lost. The upshot is that White wins an important pawn and damages Black's position.

20) White's kingside proved too vulnerable after **1...♘xf3+ 2 gxf3 ♕g3+** (using the pin on the f2-pawn) **3 ♔h1 ♕xh3+ 4 ♔g1 ♗f5** followed by ...♖h5 with mate on h2 or h1.

21) **1...♖xe3! 2 ♖xe3 ♗h6** sets up a pin. White can defend for a moment by **3 ♔d2** but Black can attack the helpless rook a second time by **3...d4**, when he ends up a piece ahead.

22) After **1 ♘xd5 exd5 2 ♖e8+ ♔g7** the b8-knight is hopelessly pinned and White only needs to attack it a second time to win it. This is achieved with **3 ♗b4** followed by ♗d6.

23) Black can exploit his dangerous and far-advanced pawn by **1...♖c1+ 2 ♖f1 ♘e3!** and thanks to the pin there's no way out for the rook on f1.

24) White sets up a pin by **1 ♖xe7! ♕xe7** and exploits it with the fork **2 ♘xd5**, when Black loses material. After **2...♘xd5 3 ♗xe7 ♘xe7 4 ♕xd7** White has won a queen for a rook.

25) White wins thanks to a double pin: **1 ♖e8! ♕xe8 2 ♘f6+** and the g-pawn is pinned against the king, while the rook is pinned so that **2...♖xf6 3 ♕xe8+** costs Black his queen.

26) Only one of the captures on c4 leads to a pin: **1...♖xc4! 2 ♖xc4 d5** and Black wins a piece. If there are several ways to make a series of exchanges, work out which sequence is best.

27) White can win Black's queen by **1 ♖b3! cxb3** (Black must take since the queen cannot move due to ♕b8#) **2 ♕xb4**. The c-pawn is pinned, so Black cannot recapture.

28) White can win by **1 ♗a2!** (not 1 ♕xd8? ♕xf2+ 2 ♔h3 ♕f1+ 3 ♔h2 ♕xb1, when Black is two pawns up) **1...♕xa2** (otherwise Black loses his queen) **2 ♕g6+ ♗g7 3 ♕xg7#**.

29) Black is threatened with mate on h8, but the clever **1...♕f2+! 2 ♔xf2 ♘g4+** uses the pin along the f-file to escape. After **3 ♔e2 ♘xh6 4 ♖xh6** Black is a piece ahead.

30) Although Black's queen is attacked, he has a lethal blow: **1...♗xe4!! 2 bxc5** (2 ♖xe4 ♖f1+ 3 ♗xf1 ♖xf1+ 4 ♔g2 ♕f2# and 2 ♗xe4 ♖f1+ 3 ♗xf1 ♖xf1+ 4 ♔g2 ♕f2# also lead to mate) **2...♖f1+ 3 ♖xf1 ♖xf1#** is mate as the g2-bishop is pinned.

31) There's no pin visible right now, but after **1 ♕h6 ♖g8 2 ♕xh7+! ♔xh7 3 ♖h3+ ♕h5 4 ♖xh5#** the g6-pawn is pinned and cannot take the rook, so it's mate.

32) Combining one tactic with another is often very effective. Here pin and fork work together to net Black's queen: **1 ♗d6+! cxd6** (1...♕xd6 2 ♘b5+ is one fork...) **2 ♖a7+ ♔b4 3 ♘c6+** ...and this is another, making use of the pin of the d7-pawn.

33) White can win brilliantly by **1 ♕g8+!! ♔xg8** (after 1...♔e7 2 ♕xf7+ ♔d6 3 ♖d1+ ♔c5 4 ♘f3 Black's king is hopelessly exposed) **2 ♘g6** and Black can only delay ♖h8# for a couple of moves. Here the crucial element was the pin of the f7-pawn.

34) This trick has won many games: **1...♖c1+ 2 ♔h2 ♖h1+! 3 ♔xh1 ♕h3+** (the g2-pawn is pinned along the b7-h1 diagonal) **4 ♔g1 ♕xg2#**.

35) **1 ♕a3+ ♕e7** (1...♔g8 2 ♗xh7+ wins the queen) **2 ♗c6!** (the black queen is pinned, and so can only move along the a3-f8 diagonal) **2...♕xa3 3 ♖xe8#**.

36) Black's king position is wide open and White wins by **1 ♕c4+ ♔d5** (1...♔f8 2 ♗b4 pins the queen) **2 ♖d1!** (exploiting the pin on the black queen) **2...♕xc4 3 ♖xd8+** (this is an example of an *in-between move* – see Chapter 8) **3...♔f7 4 bxc4** and White has won a rook.

37) The cunning **1...♕e8!** avoids material loss by counter-pinning the e5-pawn and so stops it taking on f6. Note that both 1...♖e8? and 1...♕e7? are wrong because they do not relieve the pin on the knight and in either case White replies 2 ♗e2 and the knight is lost after all.

38) **1...♕c5!** saves the knight. Not 1...♕g5? 2 ♕xg5 ♘xg5 3 h4, when the knight is lost.

39) After **1 d5** Black has a counterattack against the bishop that is pinning the knight: **1...a6 2 ♗a4** (other retreats let the knight move) **2...b5** and Black has sidestepped a disaster.

40) Black can play **1...♗xf3!** (after 1...♘xf3+? 2 gxf3 ♗e6 3 d5 Black loses the bishop). Then **2 gxf3? ♘xf3+! 3 ♕xf3 ♕xe1+** wins material for Black, so White's best is actually **2 ♕d2 ♗c6 3 dxe5 dxe5 4 ♕g5** with an equal position.

41) **1 ♘xe5! dxe5** (1...♗xd1? 2 ♗xf7+ ♔e7 3 ♘d5#) **2 ♕xg4** and White has won a pawn.

42) **1 b6+! ♔xb6** (1...♔b8 2 ♖h8+) **2 ♖h6!** and the horizontal pin prevents the rook from taking White's queen, while the vertical pin costs Black his queen after **2...♖xh6 3 ♕xe7**.

3 Skewer

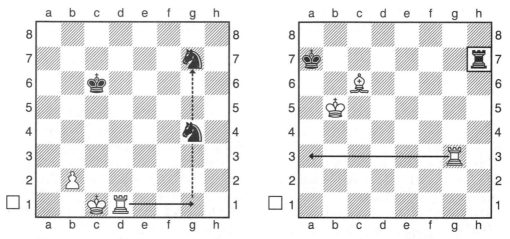

The left-hand diagram above shows the idea of a *skewer*. White plays **1 ♖g1**, attacking the knight on g4. Black is unable to defend this knight, but if it moves then the rook can take another enemy piece (here the knight on g7) that lies beyond the attacked piece. The result is that White ends up with rook and pawn against knight, a material advantage sufficient to win. As with several other tactics, only a piece that moves in straight lines can inflict a skewer, in other words a rook, bishop or queen. In this case the skewer was effective because both enemy pieces were undefended. Even if the pieces are defended, a skewer can still work provided the attacking piece is less valuable than the enemy pieces. For example, a bishop can skewer a queen and a rook even if both are defended.

Skewers don't often arise by chance and usually you have to think ahead to create one. Looking at forcing moves such as checks and captures is a great way to plan tactics in advance. The right-hand diagram is an example. There's no skewer visible in the diagram, but there are forcing moves which leave Black no choice. In particular, **1 ♖a3+** compels Black to play **1...♔b8**. Still no skewer, but there's another forcing move, **2 ♖a8+**. Once again Black has no choice: he must play **2...♔c7**. Aha! Suddenly there's the skewer **3 ♖a7+** followed by **4 ♖xh7**. Thinking ahead has won White a rook. Skewers involving a check are especially effective because a check leaves little choice.

Here are some tips for solving the exercises:

• In most of the exercises you will have to work out how to set up the skewer. Can you force the enemy king into position for a skewer? How about his queen?
• Since skewers depend on open lines, the preliminary idea is often a sacrifice to open a crucial line.
• Some exercises build on ideas developed in earlier ones. Can you use an idea you have already seen to create a winning tactic?

Exercises

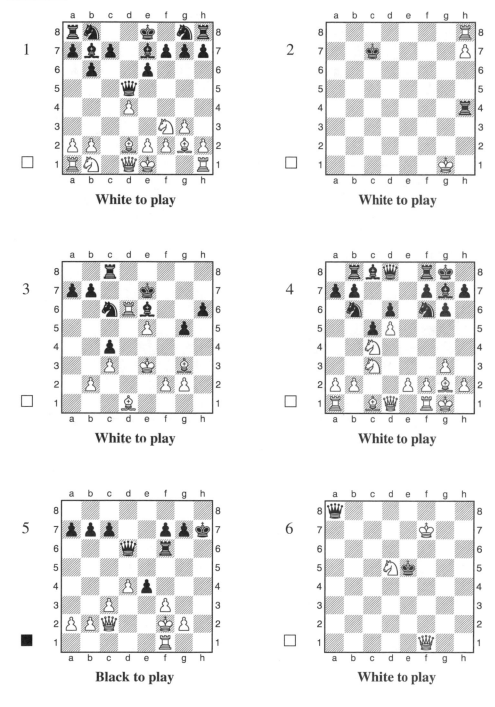

1   **White to play**

2   **White to play**

3   **White to play**

4   **White to play**

5   **Black to play**

6   **White to play**

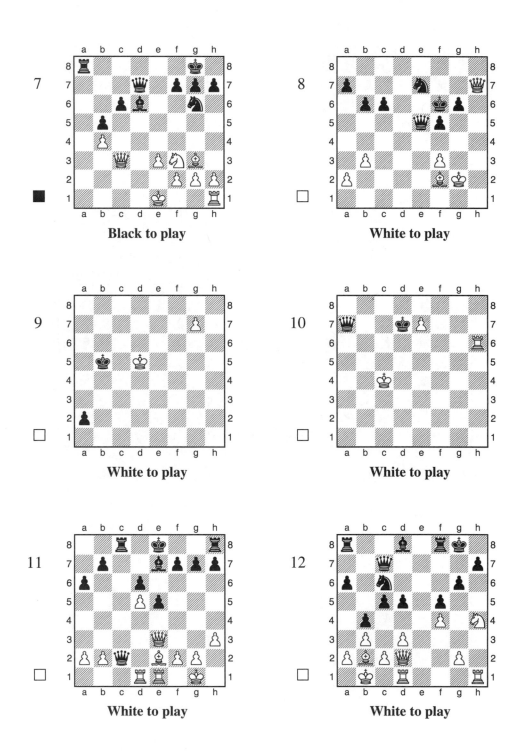

7 **Black to play**

8 **White to play**

9 **White to play**

10 **White to play**

11 **White to play**

12 **White to play**

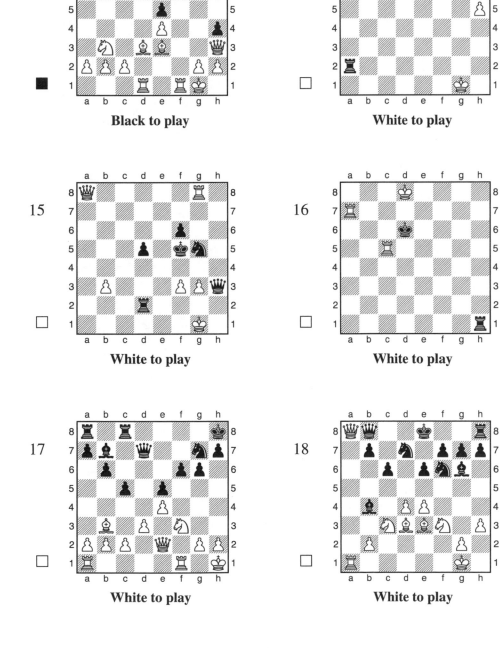

13 Black to play

14 White to play

15 White to play

16 White to play

17 White to play

18 White to play

31

Tougher Positions

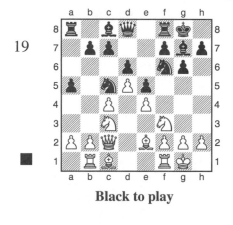

19 **Black to play**

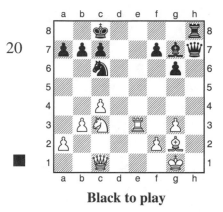

20 **Black to play**

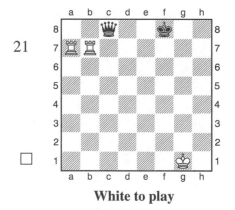

21 **White to play**

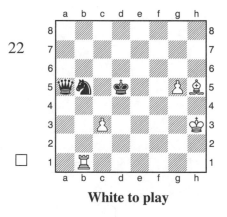

22 **White to play**

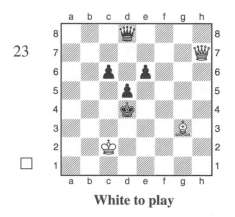

23 **White to play**

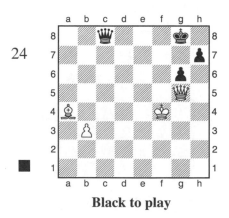

24 **Black to play**

Does the Tactic Work?

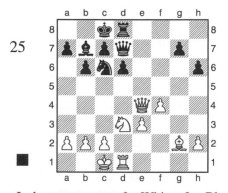

25

Is there any escape for White after Black's **1...♞a5**?

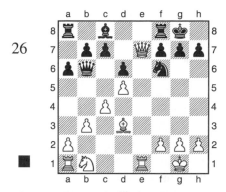

26

Is the skewer **1...♜e8** embarrassing for White?

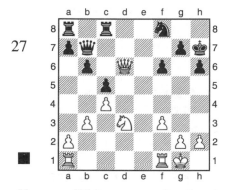

27

How can White escape after the skewer **1...♜d8**?

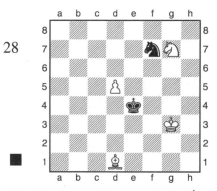

28

Can Black save the game by **1...♚xd5**?

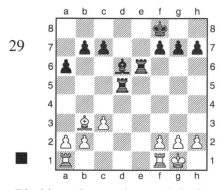

29

Black's rooks are skewered. Is there any way to avoid defeat?

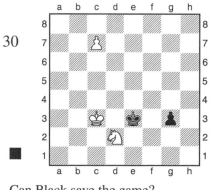

30

Can Black save the game?

Solutions to Skewer Exercises

1) Black's queen and bishop are temptingly lined up and White wins material by the *discovered attack* (see Chapter 5) **1 ♘h4**. This makes decisive gains because if the queen moves, the b7-bishop is lost. Note that the knight must move to h4 as it is necessary to defend the g2-bishop.

2) This typical endgame tactic wins the enemy rook with a skewer: **1 ♖a8!** (threatening to promote) **1...♖xh7 2 ♖a7+** and **3 ♖xh7**.

3) White wins with a sacrifice followed by a diagonal skewer: **1 ♖xe6+! ♔xe6 2 ♗g4+** followed by **3 ♗xc8**.

4) White can spring a typical opening trap: **1 ♘xd6! ♕xd6** (or else White remains a pawn ahead) **2 ♗f4** and the b8-rook falls. It's important that the black queen cannot move so as to defend the rook.

5) A quick one-two knocks White out: **1...♖xf3+!** (1...exf3 is impossible as the pawn is pinned) **2 gxf3 ♕h2+** and Black wins the queen.

6) The ending of ♕+♘ vs ♕ is normally drawn, but here is one of the exceptions: **1 ♕f4+!** (the knight sacrifice sets up a decisive skewer) **1...♔xd5 2 ♕f3+**. 1 ♕f6+? doesn't work as Black can ignore the sacrifice and play 1...♔e4.

7) White has not yet castled and Black can exploit this by **1...♗xb4! 2 ♕xb4 ♖a1+**, winning rook and pawn for bishop.

8) At the moment 1 ♕h8+? is ineffective as Black can reply 1...♔e6, but a small change in the position turns a harmless idea into a deadly one: **1 ♗d4!** (drawing the black queen away from the king) **1...♕xd4 2 ♕h8+** followed by **3 ♕xd4**.

9) It looks like a draw, but the bad position of the black king allows White to set up a skewer: **1 g8♕ a1♕ 2 ♕b8+ ♔a4** (other squares are no better) **3 ♕a7+** (or 3 ♕a8+) and **4 ♕xa1**.

10) White wins despite Black's material advantage: **1 e8♕+! ♔xe8 2 ♖h8+ ♔f7 3 ♖h7+** and **4 ♖xa7**, with an extra rook.

11) Two skewers in a row seal Black's fate: **1 ♖c1** (Black's queen must move so as to defend the rook on c8, which leaves just one possibility) **1...♕f5** and now the second skewer **2 ♗g4** finishes Black off.

12) A preliminary sacrifice opens the h-file and leads to a lethal skewer: **1 ♘xg6! hxg6 2 ♖h8+ ♔f7 3 ♖h7+** and Black loses his queen.

13) Black can chase the white queen into position for a skewer: **1...♗d7 2 ♕f3** (the only possible move for the queen) **2...♗g4** followed by **3...♗xd1**, and Black wins a rook for a bishop.

14) The skewer from Exercise 2 is concealed in this position and just one preparatory move is needed before it can be unleashed: **1 h6!** (Black must take this pawn or else White plays h7) **1...gxh6 2 ♖h8!** (this works now that the seventh rank is open) **2...♖xa7 3 ♖h7+** wins the rook.

15) The immediate 1 ♕c8+? leads to nothing after 1...♘e6 so the defensive knight must first be eliminated: **1 ♖xg5+! ♔xg5** (1...fxg5 2 ♕c8+ skewers Black straight away) **2 ♕g8+ ♔f5** (2...♔h5 3 ♕h8+ also wins the queen) **3 ♕c8+** followed by **4 ♕xh3**.

34

16) It looks like White is about to lose his extra rook, as he is threatened by both ...♔xc5 and ...♖h8#, but a clever skewer keeps his material advantage and wins: **1 ♖h5! ♖xh5 2 ♖a6+ ♔d5** (or any other square) **3 ♖a5+** and **4 ♖xh5**.

17) 1 ♘xe5! (opening up the f-file) **1...fxe5 2 ♖f7** (skewer number 1) **2...♕c6** (the only way for the queen to defend the bishop on b7) **3 ♗d5** and skewer number 2 wins material.

18) White sets up an eighth-rank skewer by nudging the black queen away from b8: **1 ♗f4!** (this bishop cannot be taken as the black queen is pinned) **1...♕xa8** (1...♕d8 2 ♕xd8+ ♔xd8 3 ♖a8+ also wins the rook) **2 ♖xa8+ ♔e7 3 ♖xh8** with an extra rook for White.

19) White should not have put his rook on b1 because it allows a typical trick, similar to Exercise 4: **1...♘fxe4!** (1...♘cxe4! is equally good) **2 ♘xe4 ♘xe4 3 ♕xe4** (or else White is just a pawn down) **3...♗f5** and the loose rook drops off.

20) After **1...♕h2+ 2 ♔f1** a queen sacrifice leads to a skewer regaining the material with interest: **2...♕h1+! 3 ♗xh1 ♖xh1+** followed by **4...♖xc1**, and Black is a piece up.

21) White can give a lot of checks with his pair of rooks, but to win he must make use of a skewer: **1 ♖f7+ ♔g8** (1...♔e8 2 ♖ae7+ ♔d8 3 ♖f8+ is similar) **2 ♖g7+ ♔h8** (2...♔f8 3 ♖af7+ ♔e8 4 ♖g8+ is another skewer) **3 ♖h7+ ♔g8 4 ♖ag7+ ♔f8 5 ♖h8+** and the queen falls.

22) Sometimes the skewer is rather well concealed. **1 ♖xb5+! ♕xb5 2 c4+!** draws Black into one of two possible skewers: **2...♔xc4 3 ♗e2+** is the first, while **2...♕xc4 3 ♗f7+** is the second.

23) Normally this material would lead to a draw, but White can win with a brilliant tactical idea: **1 ♗d6!!** (the only defence to the threat of 2 ♕d3# is to take the bishop) **1...♕xd6 2 ♕d3+ ♔c5** (2...♔e5 3 ♕g3+ is a mirror image) **3 ♕a3+** and the queen falls.

24) A rather long sequence of forcing moves leads to White losing his queen to a skewer: **1...♕c1+** (skewer number 1) **2 ♔g4 h5+ 3 ♔h4** (the only way the king can continue to guard the queen) **3...♕h1+ 4 ♔g3 ♕g1+** (skewer number 2) **5 ♔f4** (5 ♔h4 ♕h2#) **5...♕c1+** and skewer number 3 is decisive as the king can no longer move to g4.

25) 1...♘a5 can be safely met by **2 ♕g6** since the queen defends the bishop.

26) 1...♖e8?? is embarrassing only for Black as it allows a quick mate by **2 ♕xe8+ ♘xe8 3 ♖xe8#**. Here the piece delivering the skewer was not sufficiently defended.

27) 1...♖d8 is well met by **2 ♕f4!**. This indirectly defends the knight, since **2...♖xd3?** loses material to the fork **3 ♕f5+** followed by **4 ♕xd3**.

28) Even though it allows a skewer, taking the pawn is the only way for Black to save the game: **1...♔xd5! 2 ♗b3+ ♔e5 3 ♗xf7 ♔f6** and a fork wins one of the white pieces, after which White cannot win.

29) 1...♖h6! is the only move to save the game. After **2 ♗xd5 ♗xh2+ 3 ♔h1 ♗d6+** (or any other square on the same diagonal) **4 ♔g1 ♗h2+** Black draws by *perpetual check* (see Chapter 12 for more about this tactic). 1...♖h5? is wrong as 2 ♗xe6 ♗xh2+ 3 ♔h1 ♗d6+ 4 ♗h3 allows White to keep the extra rook.

30) It seems impossible to save the game because after both sides promote White has a skewer, but there is a miraculous defence: **1...g2 2 c8♕ g1♕ 3 ♕c5+ ♔e2!** and further checks don't help White, while after **4 ♕xg1** Black is stalemated.

4 Deflection and Decoy

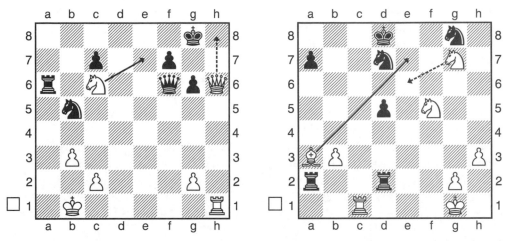

A *deflection* occurs when an enemy piece is defending a crucial square and that piece is forcibly dragged away from its responsibility. The left-hand diagram above shows the idea. Black's queen needs to defend h8 to prevent White's ♕h8#. If the black queen is pulled away from this duty then White will mate at once. A situation like this is ripe for a possible deflection, and **1 ♘e7+** is just what White needs. Black's reply **1...♕xe7** is forced, allowing **2 ♕h8#**. Pieces often have important defensive duties, so deflection is one of the most common tactical ideas in chess. It's also one of the most diverse, since the 'duty' can be almost anything, such as preventing mate (as above), stopping a pawn promoting, or simply defending another piece.

Decoy is a closely related concept. The right-hand diagram above is an example. White is a piece up, but his bishop is under attack and in addition Black threatens ...♖xg2+. Chasing the black king by 1 ♘e6+? ♚e8 2 ♘d6+ is tempting, but after 2...♚e7 it doesn't lead to anything as too many white pieces are under attack. However, **1 ♗e7+!** is fatal, as this drags the g8-knight onto a square which blocks in Black's king. After **1...♘xe7**, the idea that failed before now works spectacularly: **2 ♘e6+ ♚e8 3 ♘d6#** with a beautiful mate. The transfer of the knight from g8 to e7 harmed Black's position by taking a square away from his king. In a *deflection* it's the **departure** of an enemy piece that does the damage, whereas in a *decoy* it's the **arrival** of the piece which has dire consequences.

Here are some tips for solving the exercises:

- Look to see if an enemy piece is tied down to covering a particular square. If so, a deflection might be possible. Decoys can be harder to spot, but look for moves that force an enemy piece to a particular square. Is there then a follow-up?
- One common type of decoy involves a check (often a sacrifice) that draws the enemy king onto a bad square. Exercise 5 should give you the idea.
- In Exercise 29 you need to know that queen vs rook with no other material (apart from the kings) is generally a win.

Exercises

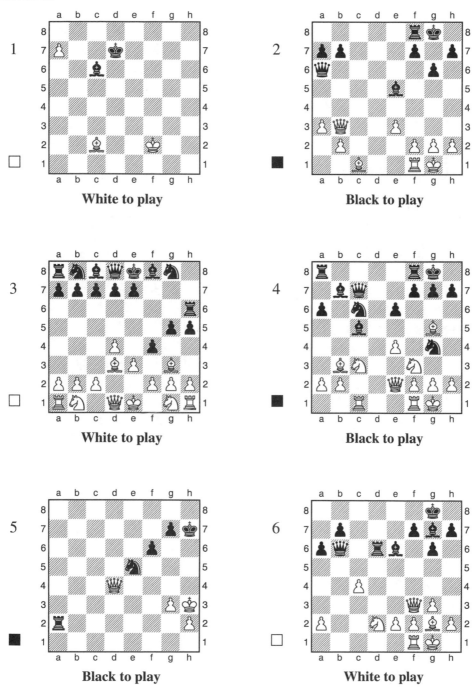

1   **White to play**

2   **Black to play**

3   **White to play**

4   **Black to play**

5   **Black to play**

6   **White to play**

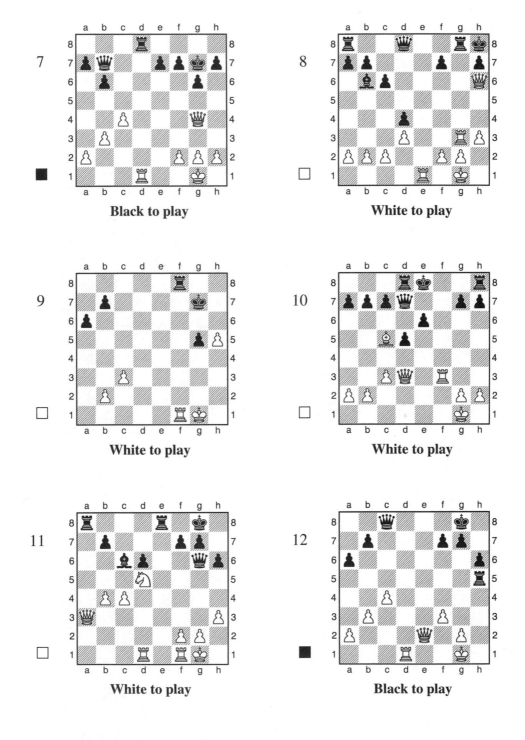

7 Black to play

8 White to play

9 White to play

10 White to play

11 White to play

12 Black to play

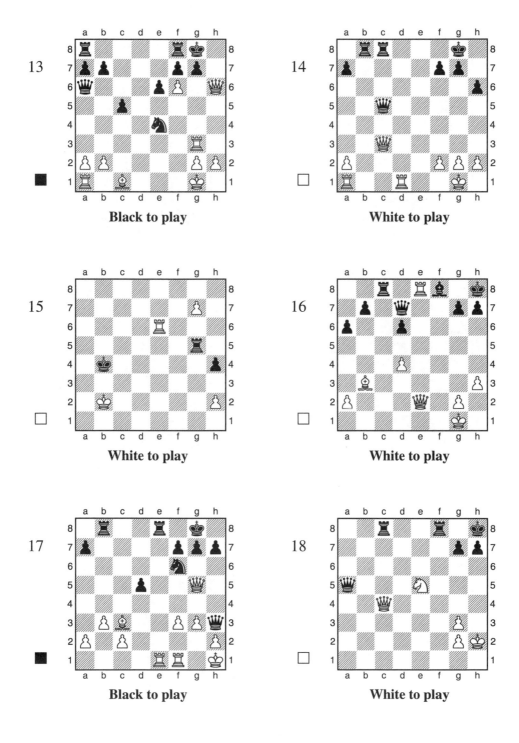

13   **Black to play**

14   **White to play**

15   **White to play**

16   **White to play**

17   **Black to play**

18   **White to play**

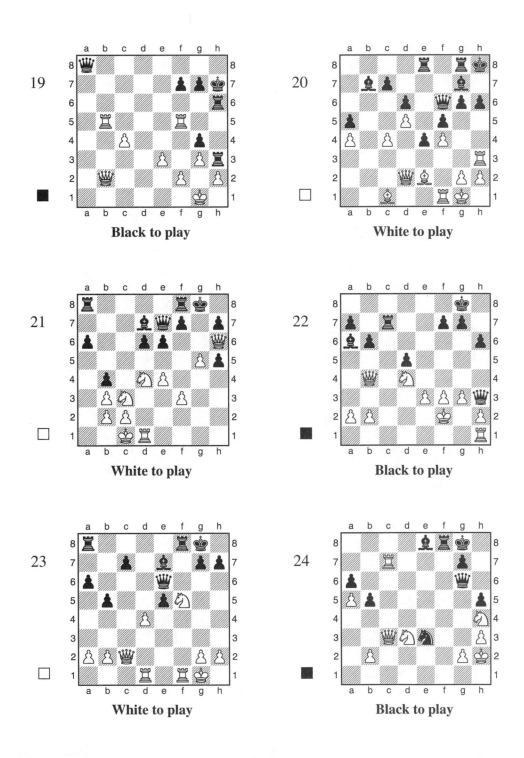

19 Black to play

20 White to play

21 White to play

22 Black to play

23 White to play

24 Black to play

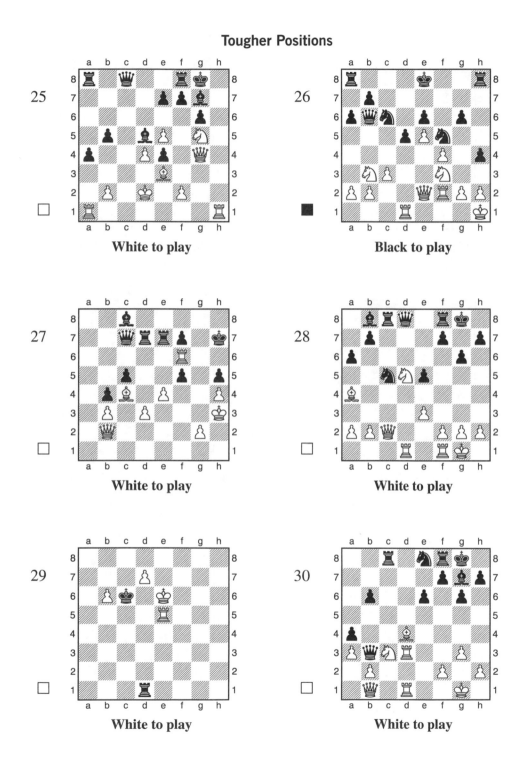

25 White to play

26 Black to play

27 White to play

28 White to play

29 White to play

30 White to play

Does the Tactic Work?

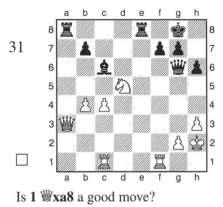

31

Is **1 ♕xa8** a good move?

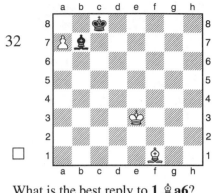

32

What is the best reply to **1 ♗a6**?

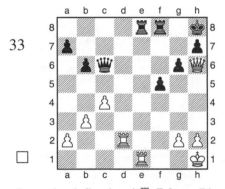

33

Does the deflection **1 ♖e7** force Black to resign?

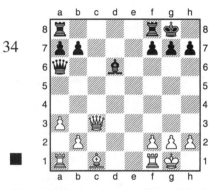

34

Should Black win material with the deflection **1...♗xh2+**?

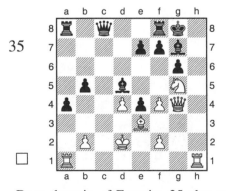

35

Does the win of Exercise 25 also work here?

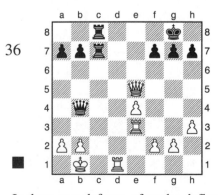

36

Is there any defence after the deflection **1...♕d2**?

Solutions to Decoy and Deflection Exercises

1) Deflection is often used to ensure the promotion of a far-advanced pawn. Here White uses a pin to deflect the enemy bishop: **1 ♗a4! ♗xa4 2 a8♕**.

2) Whenever a piece has a vital duty, you should look for a possible deflection. Here the white king must defend the f1-rook, and Black can exploit this by **1...♗xh2+! 2 ♔xh2 ♕xf1**.

3) White can deflect the h6-rook away from the mate on g6: **1 ♕xh5+! ♖xh5 2 ♗g6#**.

4) Only the f3-knight is preventing mate on h2, and **1...♘d4** eliminates that knight. White either loses his queen or gets mated after **2 ♘xd4 ♕xh2#** or **2 ♕d3 ♘xf3+** followed by **3...♕xh2#**.

5) The combination of decoy and knight fork is often deadly. Here it costs White his queen: **1...♖xh2+! 2 ♔xh2 ♘f3+**.

6) A pawn fork decoys the queen to a square which allows a knight fork: **1 c5! ♕xc5 2 ♘e4** and White will be rook for bishop up.

7) The white queen is tied to the defence of the d1-rook, and Black can exploit this with a single lethal deflection: **1...♕e4!** (other attacks on the queen are ineffective; for example, 1...h5? 2 ♕e2 is harmless) **2 ♕xe4** (or 2 ♕f3 ♕xf3 3 gxf3 ♖xd1+ and Black wins a rook) **2...♖xd1+** and mate next move.

8) White pushes his attack home with a double deflection: **1 ♖e8!** (Black's queen must defend f6, while his rook must guard g7, putting him in a fatal dilemma) **1...♕xe8** (or 1...♖xe8 2 ♕g7#) **2 ♕f6+ ♖g7 3 ♕xg7#**.

9) Black's king must guard the rook, so White can repeatedly advance his pawn with gain of time: **1 h6+ ♔g8 2 h7+** (now the pawn is far enough advanced to promote after an exchange of rooks) **2...♔g7 3 ♖xf8 ♔xf8 4 h8♕+**.

10) The h8-rook is stopping mate by ♖f8#, but can be pulled away: **1 ♕xh7! ♖xh7** (otherwise the rook is lost, leaving White a piece ahead) **2 ♖f8#**.

11) The e8-rook has the duty of preventing the knight fork ♘e7+, but it can be deflected: **1 ♕xa8!** (1 ♘e7+? ♖xe7 2 ♕xa8+ ♖e8 is wrong, as owing to the threat of mate on g2 White loses his queen) **1...♖xa8 2 ♘e7+** and White will be rook for bishop ahead.

12) After **1...♕c5+** Black either mates or wins White's queen: **2 ♕f2** (or 2 ♔f1 ♖h1#) **2...♖h1+! 3 ♔xh1 ♕xf2**.

13) It looks like mate on g7, but Black can win with a decoy: **1...♕f1+! 2 ♔xf1** (now Black can take the rook with check) **2...♘xg3+ 3 hxg3 gxh6** and Black is rook for bishop ahead.

14) This deflection idea has caught out thousands of players, including grandmasters: **1 ♖d8+!** (trying to pull Black's c8-rook away from defending the queen) **1...♔h7** (the only chance, as 1...♖xd8 2 ♕xc5 is hopeless, but it doesn't help Black) **2 ♕xc5 ♖xc5 3 ♖xb8** with an extra rook.

15) Black's rook is stopping the g7-pawn promoting, but a deflection draws it away: **1 ♖e4+** (1 ♖e7? ♖g2+ 2 ♔c1 ♔c5 is only a draw as White will soon lose the g7-pawn) **1...♔c5 2 ♖e5+! ♖xe5 3 g8♕** and wins.

16) Black's position looks fragile, but there is only one way to demolish it: **1 ♕c4!** (threatening mate on g8 and attacking the c8-rook) **1...♖xc4** (now the black rook no longer defends the bishop on f8) **2 ♖xf8#**.

17) Although it's only two moves deep, even grandmasters have missed this type of tactic. The e1-rook must defend its neighbour, setting the stage for a deadly deflection: **1...Re2!** (threatening mate on h2 or g2) **2 Rxe2 Qxf1#**.

18) This position features the classic decoy scenario, *smothered mate*. **1 Nf7+ Kg8** (1...Rxf7 2 Qxc8+ mates in two more moves) **2 Nh6++** (*double check*, so Black must move his king – see Chapter 6) **2...Kh8 3 Qg8+!** (the key point: White decoys the rook so that it blocks the king's flight-square on g8, but there is also a deflection element as the rook will no longer control f7) **3...Rxg8 4 Nf7#**.

19) A decoy allows the doubled black rooks to join the attack with check: **1...Qh1+!** (1...Rxh2? 2 Kf1 Rh1+ 3 Ke2 is only equal) **2 Kxh1 Rxh2+ 3 Kg1 Rh1+ 4 Kg2 R6h2#**.

20) First, the queen is decoyed to the vulnerable square b2 by **1 Bb2! Qxb2** (1...Qf7 2 Rxh6#). Then the bishop is deflected away from the queen's defence by **2 Rxh6+! Bxh6 3 Qxb2+** and White even picks up the bishop on b7 at the end. Swapping the moves round by 1 Rxh6+? Bxh6 2 Bb2 doesn't work, as Black can return the extra rook by 2...Re5, blocking the long diagonal.

21) Sacrificing one knight eliminates Black's guard of d5, allowing the other knight to jump in and decide the game: **1 Nf5! exf5 2 Nd5 Qe6 3 Nf6+ Qxf6 4 gxf6** followed by **5 Qg7#**.

22) A surprising move draws the h1-rook away from the defence of the pawn on h2: **1...Bf1!** (threatening 2...Qg2+ 3 Ke1 Rc1#) **2 Rxf1** (or 2 Rg1 Qxh2+ 3 Kf1 Rc1+) **2...Qxh2+ 3 Ke1 Rc1#**.

23) A cunning trick involving an *in-between move* (see Chapter 8) nets White a piece: **1 Qb3!** (pinning the undefended queen and drawing it away from the defence of the e7-bishop) **1...Qxb3** (1...Rf6 2 Nxe7+ also wins for White) **2 Nxe7+ Kh8** (Black cannot play 2...Kf7 because that square is controlled by the f1-rook) **3 axb3**.

24) A spectacular decoy decides the game at once: **1...Qg3+!! 2 Kxg3** (or 2 Kg1 Rf1#) **2...Nf1#**.

25) The attack along the h-file looks dangerous, but there is only one way to finish Black off: **1 Rh8+!** (1 Qh4? is tempting, but after 1...Rd8 2 Qh7+ Kf8 there is no win for White) **1...Bxh8** (or 1...Kxh8 2 Qh4+ Kg8 3 Qh7#) **2 Qh4** (the decoy of the bishop to h8 has undermined the defence Black used against 1 Qh4?) **2...Rd8 3 Qh7+ Kf8 4 Qxh8#**.

26) An initial sacrifice opens the h-file, but the real killer move is a deflection: **1...Ng3+!** (forking king and queen, so White must take) **2 hxg3 hxg3+ 3 Kg1 gxf2+ 4 Qxf2**. Now the white king must defend the queen, but **4...Rh1+!** draws the king away and wins the queen after **5 Kxh1 Qxf2**.

27) Black's king is forced to run the gauntlet after a rook sacrifice deflects it away from control of h8: **1 Rh6+! Kxh6 2 Qh8+** (the queen enters the attack with check) **2...Kg6 3 exf5+ Kxf5 4 Qxh5+** and it's mate after **4...Kf6 5 Qg5#** or **4...Kf4 5 Qg5#**.

28) A short but intricate tactic wins material: **1 Bd7!** (the c8-rook is trapped, so Black must take the bishop) **1...Nxd7** (1...Rxd7 2 Nf6+ wins the queen) **2 Qxc8!** (a further sacrifice sets up a knight fork) **2...Qxc8 3 Ne7+ Kg7 4 Nxc8 Rxc8 5 Rxd7** and White is material up.

29) White is two pawns ahead, but both pawns are vulnerable. The only way to win is to sacrifice the rook to deflect the black king away from control of b7: **1 ♖c5+!!** (1 b7? ♖d6+! is a draw after 2 ♔e7 ♖xd7+ or 2 ♔f5 ♔xb7 3 ♖e7 ♖c6) **1...♔xc5** (1...♔xb6 2 ♖c8 promotes the d-pawn after Black's checks run out; for example, 2...♖e1+ 3 ♔f5 ♖f1+ 4 ♔e4 ♖e1+ 5 ♔f3 ♖f1+ 6 ♔e2) **2 b7** (now Black cannot stop both pawns) **2...♖d6+** (White also wins after 2...♖e1+ 3 ♔f7 ♖f1+ 4 ♔e8 ♖e1+ 5 ♔d8 ♖b1 6 ♔c7) **3 ♔e7 ♖b6 4 d8♕** wins, since queen vs rook is a win in general.

30) White wins with an unusual combination involving two *discovered attacks* and a decoy: **1 ♘d5!!** (the first discovered attack hits the queen and threatens ♘e7+, so Black's reply is forced) **1...♕xd5** (the queen has been decoyed to a vulnerable square, allowing White to unleash a second discovered attack) **2 ♗xg7 ♕f5 3 ♗xf8** and White finishes rook for knight (and pawn) ahead.

31) **1 ♕xa8?** loses the queen as **1...♕d6+** cuts out the fork on e7 with gain of time. After **2 ♔h1 ♖xa8** Black is queen for rook up.

32) After **1 ♗a6** the only move to avoid defeat is **1...♔c7!**, calmly unpinning the bishop. Then the pawn is lost following **2 ♗xb7 ♔xb7** or **2 ♔d4 ♔b6**, when the game is a draw.

33) After **1 ♖e7?** (1 ♖de2 is better) Black has the defence **1...♖f7!** preventing the mates on g7 and h7. Then 2 ♖xf7?? is impossible due to 2...♖e1#, so White has to be content with **2 ♖xe8+** (2 ♖de2 looks awkward, but 2...♖d8! is a good reply) **2...♕xe8 3 ♕h4** with an equal position.

34) **1...♗xh2+?** is actually a blunder, since **2 ♔xh2 ♕xf1 3 ♗h6** threatens mate on g7 and so wins Black's queen.

35) **1 ♖h8+ ♗xh8 2 ♕h4** doesn't win, since there is a crucial difference compared to Exercise 25. Here White does not control f6, so the black king can slip away by **2...♔g7!**. Then White's attack dies out; for example, **3 ♕h7+ ♔f6 4 ♕h4 ♕f5** and Black wins with his extra rook.

36) **1...♕d2?** appears terrifying, since 2 ♖xd2?? ♖c1# and 2 ♖ee1?? ♕c2+ 3 ♔a1 ♕c1+ 4 ♖xc1 ♖xc1+ 5 ♖xc1 ♖xc1# both lead to mate. There is only one defence: the counter-deflection **2 ♕e8+! ♖xe8** (now there is no mate on c1 and White can safely take the queen) **3 ♖xd2** gives White an advantage since he is a pawn up in the ending.

DECOY

45

5 Discovered Attack

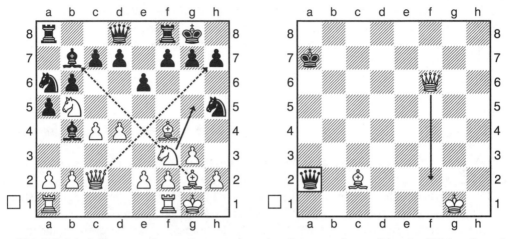

The left-hand diagram above demonstrates the *discovered attack* tactic. White plays **1 ♘g5!**. The knight move creates a threat of 2 ♕xh7#, but at the same time unveils an attack by the g2-bishop against the undefended bishop on b7. Black must deal with the mate threat and then White plays **2 ♗xb7**, winning a piece. This is the essence of a discovered attack: one of your pieces (the *front* piece) moves with a threat, at the same time uncovering an attack from a friendly piece (the *rear* piece) located behind. We say that the move *discovers* an attack by the rear piece. It's often impossible for the opponent to counter both threats at the same time. The front piece can be any chess piece, but the rear piece has to be a piece that moves along straight lines, in other words a queen, rook or bishop.

The discovered attack is especially effective when the front piece delivers check. Since a check requires an immediate counter, the rear piece is then generally free to do some damage. In the right-hand diagram above, Black is subjected to torture by discovered attack. Normally a queen and bishop do not beat a queen when there is no other material on the board, but in this particular position White wins by **1 ♕f2+!**. The idea is to set up a possible discovered attack against the black queen. Indeed, if White can now move his bishop with check, he will win Black's queen. This happens after **1...♔a8 2 ♗e4+**, **1...♔b7 2 ♗e4+** and **1...♔a6 2 ♗d3+**, so Black cannot move his king to a light square. The only remaining move is **1...♔b8**, but then White wins by **2 ♕b6+ ♔c8** (2...♔a8 3 ♗e4+ also mates) **3 ♗f5+** and mate next move.

Here are some tips for solving the exercises:

- Is there already a line-up of pieces that might allow a discovered attack? If not, can you create one?
- Sometimes the threat by the rear piece is not to capture an enemy piece, but to deliver mate.
- There are cases in which an apparently pinned piece can move, turning the pin into a discovered attack. For this to work, the piece that moves must create a really strong threat (Exercise 7 is one example).

Exercises

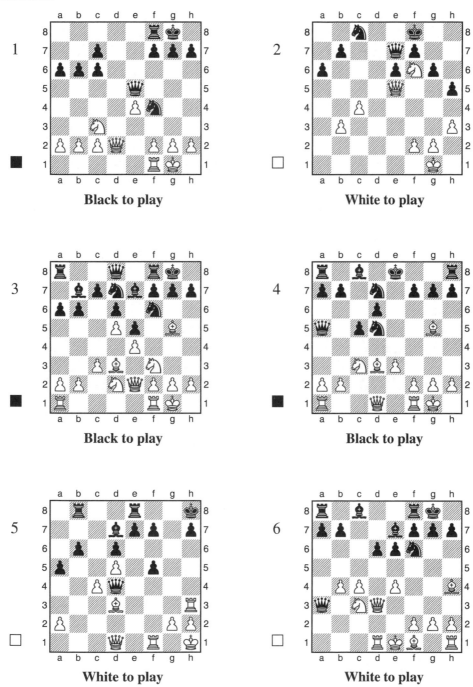

1   **Black to play**

2   **White to play**

3   **Black to play**

4   **Black to play**

5   **White to play**

6   **White to play**

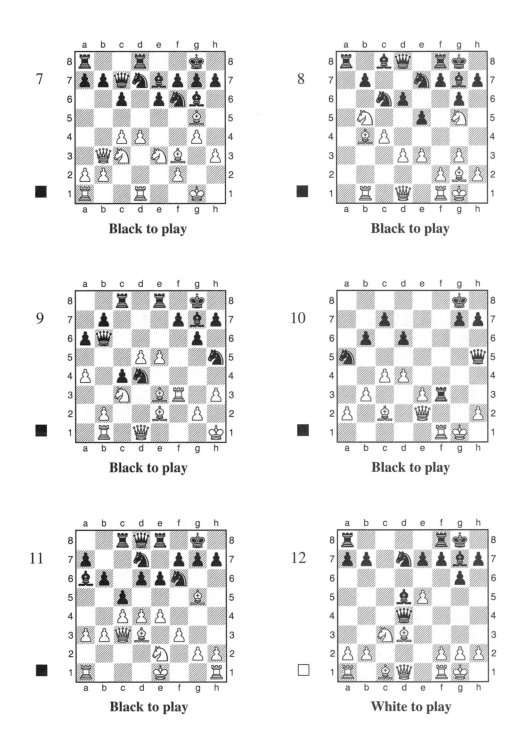

7   **Black to play**

8   **Black to play**

9   **Black to play**

10   **Black to play**

11   **Black to play**

12   **White to play**

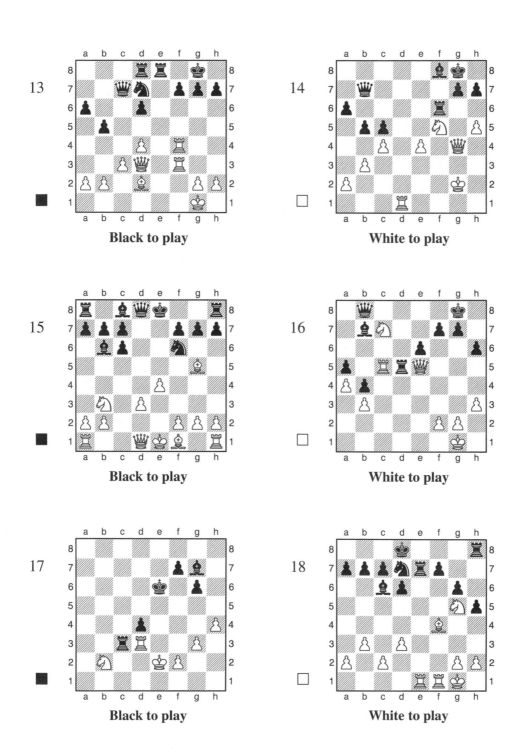

13 **Black to play**

14 **White to play**

15 **Black to play**

16 **White to play**

17 **Black to play**

18 **White to play**

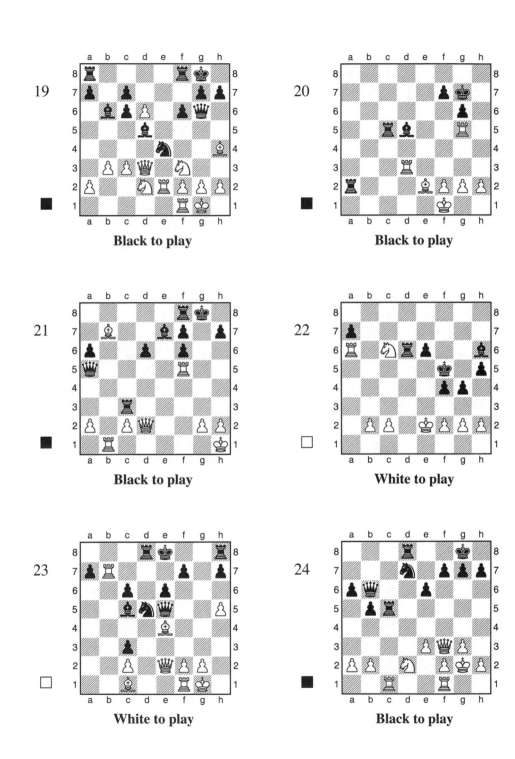

19   **Black to play**

20   **Black to play**

21   **Black to play**

22   **White to play**

23   **White to play**

24   **Black to play**

Tougher Positions

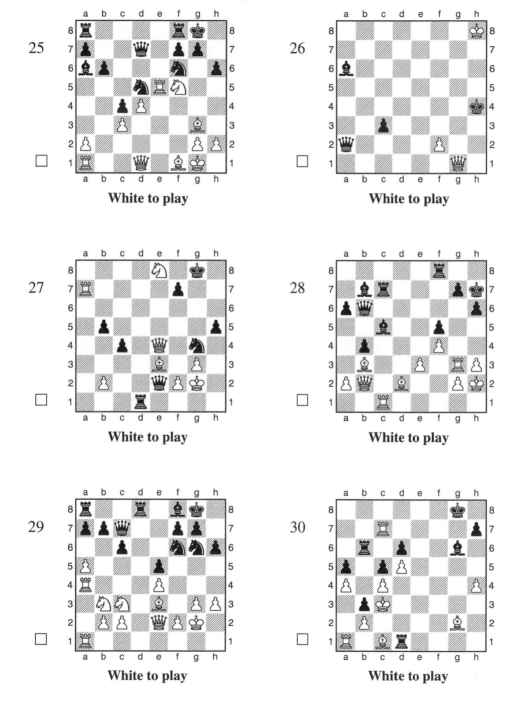

25 White to play

26 White to play

27 White to play

28 White to play

29 White to play

30 White to play

Does the Tactic Work?

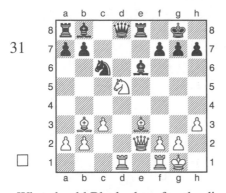

31

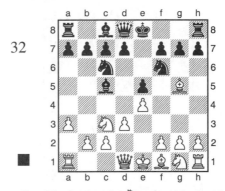

32

What should Black play after the discovered attack **1 ♘b6**?

Can Black play **1...♘xe4**, with the idea **2 ♗xd8 ♗xf2+ 3 ♔e2 ♘d4#**?

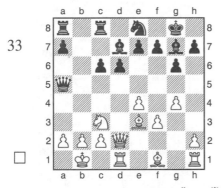

33

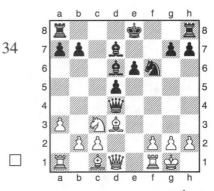

34

Can White win a pawn with **1 ♘d5 ♛xd2 2 ♘xe7+** followed by **3 ♖xd2**?

Does the discovered attack **1 ♗g6+** win the game?

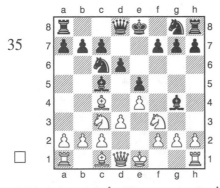

35

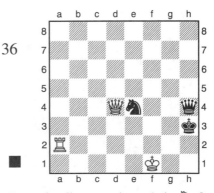

36

White played **1 ♗xf7+**, to meet **1...♔xf7** by **2 ♘g5+** and **3 ♛xg4**. Does this work?

Does the discovered attack **1...♘g3+** win for Black?

52

Solutions to Discovered Attack Exercises

1) **1...♕g5!** creates a double threat of 2...♕xg2# and the discovered attack 2...♘h3+, winning the queen. White cannot meet both threats.

2) **1 ♘d5!** discovers an attack, not against an enemy piece, but against the square h8 where White threatens ♕h8#. Since it also attacks Black's queen there is no defence; for example, **1...exd5 2 ♕h8#** or **1...f6 2 ♘xe7 fxe5 3 ♘xc8**, winning a piece.

3) Black wins a pawn with a typical 'elastic band' trick in which the knight first jumps forward by **1...♘xd5!** and then springs back after **2 ♗xe7** (2 exd5 ♗xg5 also costs White a pawn) **2...♘xe7**.

4) Undefended pieces, such as the g5-bishop here, can easily become a target for tactics. In this case **1...♘xc3** (playing 1...c4? first doesn't work, since 2 ♗f5 ♘xc3 3 ♕xd6! threatens mate on e7 and leads to an equal position) **2 bxc3 c4** attacks both white bishops and wins a piece.

5) An initial sacrifice draws the black king onto a square which allows a discovered attack: **1 ♖xh7+! ♔xh7** (1...♔g8 2 ♕h5 gives White a decisive attack against the exposed black king) **2 ♗xf5+ ♗xf5 3 ♕xd4** and White wins.

6) White wins with a typical discovered attack plus *in-between move* tactic (see also Chapter 8): **1 ♘d5!** (attacking a3 and e7) **1...♕xd3 2 ♘xe7+** (this is the in-between move, played after Black takes the white queen, but before White recaptures) **2...♔h8 3 ♗xd3** and White keeps his extra piece as Black cannot trap the e7-knight. For example, **3...♗d7 4 ♗c2 ♖fe8 5 e5! dxe5 6 ♗xf6 gxf6 7 ♖xd7** and White even wins another piece.

7) The pin on the f6-knight is more apparent than real. Black gains material by **1...♘xg4! 2 hxg4** (the point is that 2 ♗xe7 allows 2...♕h2+ 3 ♔f1 ♕xf2#) **2...♗xg5**, winning a pawn for nothing. The pin backfired on White because the f6-knight was able to move and create a stronger threat than taking on e7. What looked like a pin for White actually turned into a discovered attack for Black.

8) **1...♘xb4 2 ♖xb4 ♘c6** sets up a double attack against b4 and g5. The only way to meet this is by **3 ♗xc6**, but then **3...bxc6** brings about a further double attack against b5 and g5.

9) The d4-knight appears pinned against the queen, but this is an optical illusion: **1...♘xf3!** (Black grabs the rook and cheerfully offers his queen) **2 ♗xb6 ♘g3#**.

10) Black wins with a discovered attack followed by a deflection: **1...♖g3+! 2 ♔f2** (the only way to avoid immediate loss of the queen) **2...♖g2+ 3 ♔xg2 ♕xe2+** and Black wins.

11) Another pin that is not a pin. The f6-knight appears pinned, but Black can turn the line-up of queen on d8 and bishop on g5 to his advantage using a discovered attack: **1...♘xe4!** and Black wins a pawn after **2 ♗xe4 ♕xg5** or **2 ♗xd8 ♘xc3 3 ♘xc3 ♖cxd8**.

12) **1 ♗b5!** (directly attacking the d7-knight and at the same time discovering an attack along the d-file) **1...♕xd1 2 ♖xd1** attacks two black pieces and wins one; for example, **2...♗c6 3 ♗xc6 bxc6 4 ♖xd7**.

13) **1...♘e5!** (forking queen and rook) **2 dxe5 dxe5** (now it's the queen and the other rook under attack) **3 ♖xf7** (relatively best) **3...♕xf7! 4 ♖xf7 ♖xd3** and Black has won rook for bishop.

14) A preliminary decoy draws the black queen onto the same diagonal as White's queen, setting up a discovered attack similar to Exercise 1: **1 ♖d7! ♕xd7** (Black must take, or else 2 ♖xg7+ wins) **2 ♘h6+ ♖xh6 3 ♕xd7** and White has enough extra material to win. For example, **3...♖xh5 4 ♕e6+ ♔h8 5 ♕f7** decides the game at once.

15) The pin on the f6-knight backfires for White after **1...♘xe4!**, since **2 ♗xd8** leads to mate by **2...♗xf2+ 3 ♔e2 ♗g4#**. Instead White should cut his losses with 2 dxe4 ♕xg5, restricting Black to the gain of a pawn.

16) Two discovered attacks in a row seal Black's fate: **1 ♘xd5!** (discovering an attack on Black's queen) **1...♕xe5 2 ♘e7+** (and now a second discovered attack regains the material with interest) **2...♔f8 3 ♖xe5 ♔xe7 4 ♖xa5** with an easy win for White.

17) **1...♖c2+ 2 ♖d2 ♖xb2!** (not 2...d3+? 3 ♘xd3, when White wins a pawn instead of losing a piece) **3 ♖xb2 d3+** (here is the discovered attack) **4 ♔xd3 ♗xb2** and Black is a piece for a pawn up with a winning position.

18) **1 ♘xf7+! ♖xf7** (now that the white and black rooks are lined up along the f-file, the stage is set for a discovered attack) **2 ♗g5+ ♘f6** (2...♔c8 3 ♖xf7 is just as bad) **3 ♗xf6+ ♖xf6 4 ♖xf6** and White is rook for bishop ahead.

19) **1...♘g3!** (attacking both the e2-rook and the queen on d3) **2 ♕xg6 ♘xe2+** (an *in-between move*) **3 ♔h1 hxg6** and Black has won a rook.

20) The undefended rook on g5 proves White's undoing: **1...♖a1+ 2 ♗d1** (2 ♖d1 ♖xd1+ 3 ♗xd1 ♗c4+ is even worse) **2...♖xd1+! 3 ♖xd1 ♗c4+** followed by **4...♖xg5**, and Black wins a piece.

21) Black's queen is under attack, but he can win with the discovered attack **1...♖b3!** (1...♕xf5? 2 ♕xc3 is only equal); for example, **2 axb3 ♕xd2** or **2 ♕xa5 ♖xb1+** mating.

22) This time it's a mixture of discovered attack and deflection: **1 ♘e7+** (attacking the rook, so Black's reply is forced to avoid immediate loss of the rook) **1...♔e5 2 ♘g6+** (Black's poor king is chased along its fourth rank until it finally loses contact with the rook) **2...♔d5 3 c4+! ♔c5 4 b4+** and White wins the rook.

23) **1 ♗g6!!** (a surprising discovered attack against Black's queen) **1...♕xe2** (1...♕f6 2 ♖xf7 is also hopeless for Black) **2 ♗xf7+ ♔f8 3 ♗h6#**.

24) **1...♘e5** (this discovered attack strikes at both f3 and d2) **2 ♕e2** (or 2 ♕d1 ♖cd5 3 ♖c2 ♕d6 and the pin along the d-file wins a piece) **2...♘c6+** is a crushing fork since White must deal with the check, after which Black simply takes on c1.

25) This is a refined version of the idea from Exercise 1. **1 ♖xd5! ♘xd5** (forced, since 1...♕xd5 2 ♘e7+ loses the queen to a fork) **2 ♕g4!** (threatening mate on g7) **2...f6** (2...g6 3 ♘xh6+ is the same) **3 ♘xh6+** and the discovered attack wins Black's queen.

26) Discovered attacks are possible even when there are few pieces on the board: **1 ♕h2+! ♔g5** (1...♔g4 2 f3+ comes to the same thing) **2 f4+** and White wins the enemy queen.

27) Black has a dangerous attack and threatens 1...♘xe3+ 2 ♕xe3 ♕f1+ 3 ♔f3 ♖d3, so White must act immediately: **1 ♘f6+! ♘xf6 2 ♖a8+ ♔g7** (now the black king is on a dark square and White cuts loose with a discovered attack picking up Black's queen) **3 ♗h6+ ♔xh6 4 ♕xe2** and White wins.

28) The discovered attack is well-hidden in this position. **1 ♖xc5! ♕xc5** (1...♖xc5 2 ♕xg7# makes use of the deflection of Black's rook) **2 ♗xb4!** (skewering the queen and the rook on f8; if Black does not take the bishop then he will be a piece down) **2...♕xb4 3 ♗g8+** (the discovered attack) **3...♔xg8 4 ♕xb4** and White has won queen and pawn for rook and bishop, a decisive material advantage. This position is typical in that several tactical elements combine to make the whole thing work: deflection, decoy of the queen to b4, skewer and discovered attack.

29) This tactic is based on a discovered attack along the a-file: **1 ♗b6! axb6** (or else White wins the d8-rook in return for his bishop) **2 axb6** (now queen and rook are under attack) **2...♕xb6** (2...♖xa4 3 bxc7 is even worse as White threatens to promote his pawn on d8) **3 ♖xa8** and here too White has won rook for bishop.

30) Black has the crushing threat of ...♖d3#, so White looks to be in trouble despite his extra piece. However, he has a cunning defence which not only saves but even wins the game: **1 ♖c8+** (1 ♖g7+? ♔xg7 2 ♗h6+ ♔xh6 3 ♖xd1 is only equal) **1...♔f7 2 ♖f8+!** (now Black's king must move to a dark square, allowing a discovered attack) **2...♔xf8** (2...♔e7 3 ♗g5+ and 2...♔g7 3 ♗h6+ are no better) **3 ♗h6+ ♔f7 4 ♖xd1** and the mate threat has gone, leaving White a safe piece ahead.

31) **1 ♘b6??** is a mistake due to **1...♕c7** winning a piece. White must deal with the threatened mate by ...♕h2# and then Black can simply play 2...axb6.

32) **1...♘xe4??** is a blunder which loses a piece after **2 ♘xe4**, defending the bishop on g5.

33) **1 ♘d5?** does not win a pawn. After **1...♕xd2 2 ♘xe7+ ♔f8** Black attacks the knight and wins a piece for two pawns even after the relatively best **3 ♘xg6+ hxg6 4 ♖xd2**.

34) **1 ♗g6+?** does not win because after **1...hxg6 2 ♕xd4 ♗xh2+ 3 ♔h1 ♗e5+** Black regains the queen with a *discovered check* (see Chapter 6) and ends up a piece ahead.

35) **1 ♗xf7+? ♔xf7 2 ♘g5+** doesn't work because Black plays **2...♕xg5! 3 ♗xg5 ♗xd1 4 ♖xd1** and keeps an extra piece.

36) **1...♘g3+** doesn't win. After **2 ♔e1** (2 ♔g1? ♕xd4+ takes the queen with check) **2...♕xd4** White has a miraculous draw by **3 ♖h2+! ♔g4** (3...♔xh2 is stalemate) **4 ♖h4+** and now Black must play **4...♔xh4** to avoid losing his queen, but then White is again stalemated.

DISCOVERED ATTACK

6 Discovered and Double Check

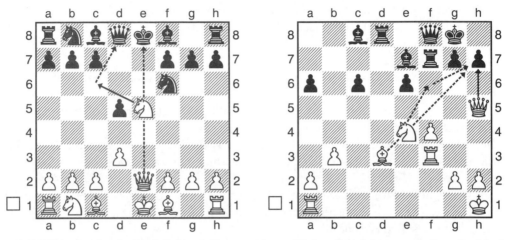

It is White to play in the left-hand diagram above. If the e5-knight moves, then the black king will be in check from the queen on e2. We say that the knight has *discovered check* from the queen. In a discovered check, the rear piece (here the queen) must be one of the chess pieces that moves in straight lines: a queen, rook or bishop. The *front piece* (here the knight) can be any piece apart from a queen, including a pawn or even, in rare cases, the king.

A discovered check is powerful because the front piece effectively gets a free move. The move by the front piece gives a check from the rear piece, which has to be dealt with, and then you can move the front piece again. If you have the possibility of a discovered check, try to do as much damage as possible with the front piece, keeping in mind that in most cases **you will have two moves with it**. In the above position, **1 ♘c6+** is the most destructive knight move. Black must respond to the check, and then the knight takes Black's queen. **1...♕e7** doesn't help Black, as the knight can take the queen in any case.

A *double check* is one step up from a discovered check. This is a discovered check in which the move of the front piece also checks the enemy king, so that the king is in check from both the rear piece and the front piece. In the right-hand diagram above, White plays **1 ♕xh7+!** (not 1 ♘f6+? gxf6, when Black defends h7) **1...♔xh7 2 ♘f6++**. Here's the double check, with the black king under attack from both the d3-bishop and the f6-knight. Although both these pieces are under threat, Black cannot take either because he would still be in check from the other piece. Because of this, **a double check can only be answered by a king move**. Black must play either **2...♔h6** or **2...♔h8**, and both are met by **3 ♖h3#**.

Here are some tips for solving the exercises:

- If there is no discovered check in the diagram, you will have to set one up, often by an exchange or sacrifice that opens a line towards the enemy king.
- Choosing the right square for the front piece is often crucial.
- If a discovered check isn't good enough, try to find a double check instead.

Exercises

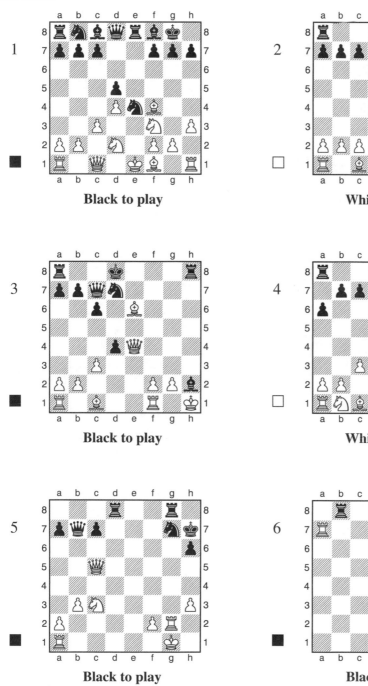

1   **Black to play**

2   **White to play**

3   **Black to play**

4   **White to play**

5   **Black to play**

6   **Black to play**

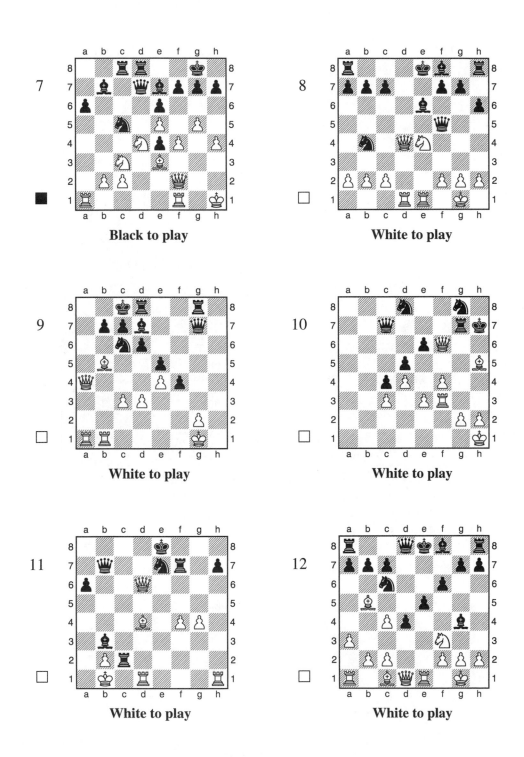

7 Black to play

8 White to play

9 White to play

10 White to play

11 White to play

12 White to play

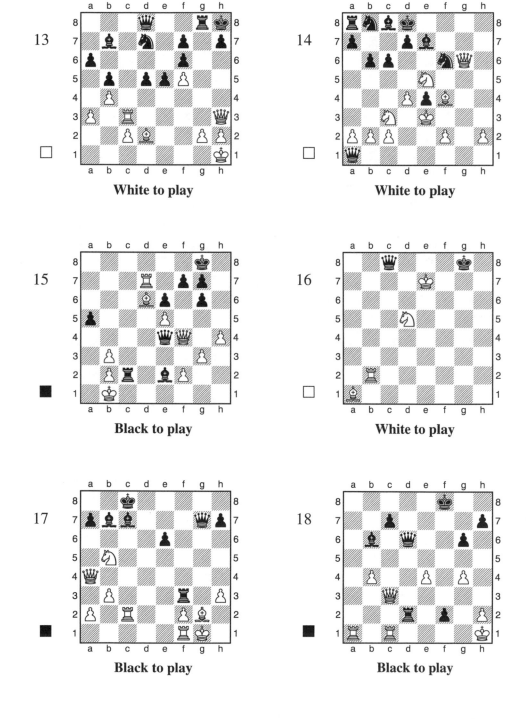

13

White to play

14

White to play

15

Black to play

16

White to play

17

Black to play

18

Black to play

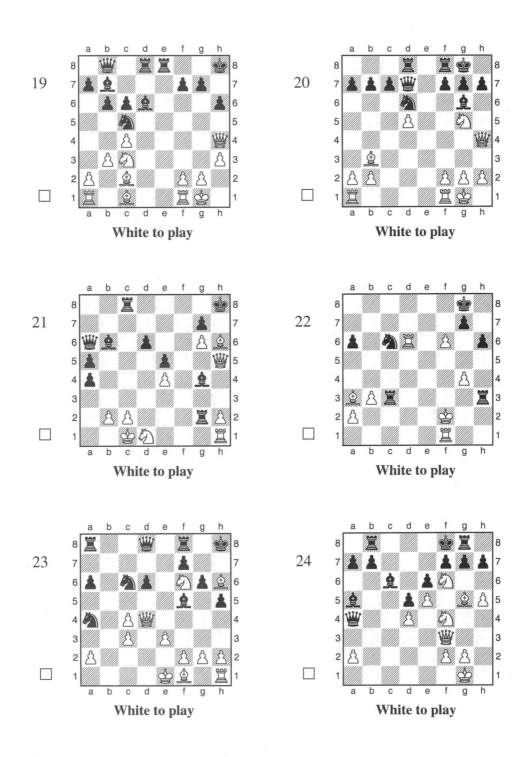

19 White to play

20 White to play

21 White to play

22 White to play

23 White to play

24 White to play

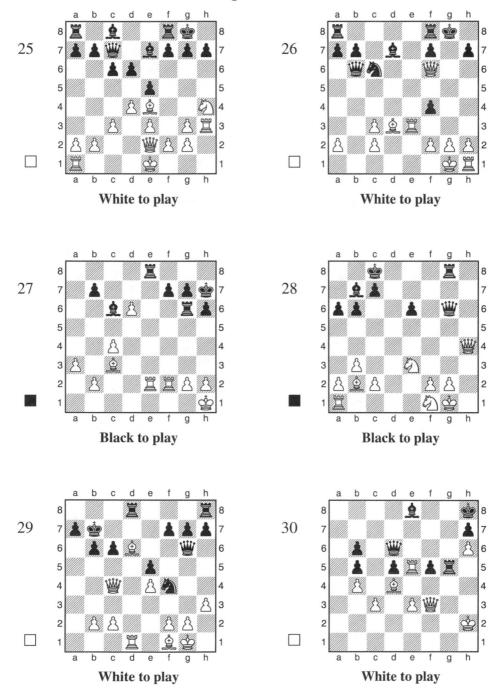

25 White to play

26 White to play

27 Black to play

28 Black to play

29 White to play

30 White to play

Does the Tactic Work?

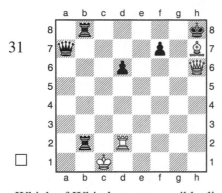

31

Which of White's many possible discovered checks is correct?

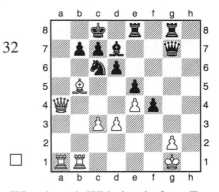

32

Why doesn't White's win from Exercise 9 work here?

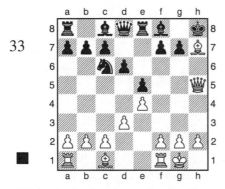

33

White is threatening a deadly discovered check. What should Black play?

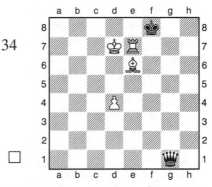

34

Which is better, **1 ♖f7+ ♔g8 2 ♖f1+** or **1 ♖e8+ ♔g7 2 ♖g8+**?

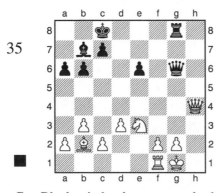

35

Can Black win by the same method as in Exercise 28?

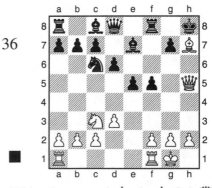

36

White threatens **1 ♗g6+ ♔g8 2 ♕h7#**. How can Black save the game?

Solutions to Discovered and Double Check Exercises

1) If you have a choice of discovered checks, look for the one that wins the most material. Here the most destructive check leads to the win of a whole rook: **1...♘g3+** followed by **2...♘xh1**. Other discovered checks win no more than a pawn.

2) White wins a piece by **1 ♗xf5** since if **1...♗xf5** then Black loses his queen to the discovered check **2 ♘c6+** (2 ♘g6+ picks up a rook but is not as good as winning the queen).

3) It's worth knowing this idea, since it often occurs in practical play. A discovered check clears the h2-square and leads to mate: **1...♗g1+! 2 ♔xg1** (or 2 ♔h3 ♕h2#) **2...♕h2#**.

4) White can win a piece by **1 ♕xf5!** since **1...♘xf5 2 ♗b5#** gives double check and mate!

5) Black's rook is on the same file as the white king, setting the stage for a discovered check: **1...♕xg2+! 2 ♔xg2 ♘e6+** and **3...♘xc5**, when Black has won a rook.

6) Black's rook, knight and h-pawn work together to weave a mating-net around the white king: **1...♖b1+ 2 ♔h2 ♘f1+ 3 ♔g1 ♘g3+!** (this discovered check is the key move) **4 ♔h2 ♖h1#**.

7) The e3-bishop is the only thing preventing the crushing ...e3+, so Black sacrifices his queen to lift the blockade: **1...♕xd4! 2 ♗xd4 e3+ 3 ♕g2 ♗xg2+ 4 ♔xg2 ♖xd4** and Black has won a piece.

8) A queen sacrifice blasts the way open to Black's king: **1 ♕d7+!** (1 ♘f6+? is tempting since 1...♕xf6? allows 2 ♕d7# but 1...♔e7 2 ♕xb4+ ♔xf6 allows Black to wriggle out) **1...♗xd7 2 ♘f6++** (not 2 ♘d6++? ♔d8 3 ♖e8+ due to 3...♗xe8 – the bishop must be pinned or it is not mate) **2...♔d8 3 ♖e8#**.

9) White pushes his attack home with a neat finish involving a queen sacrifice to draw Black's king into a lethal discovered check: **1 ♕a8+ ♘b8 2 ♕xb7+! ♔xb7 3 ♗xd7#**.

10) White's queen is under threat, but Black's king is vulnerable to a discovered check: **1 ♖h3! ♘xf6** (or 1...♘h6 2 ♕xh6+! ♔xh6 and now 3 ♗f7# or 3 ♗e8#) **2 ♗f7+ ♘h5 3 ♖xh5#**.

11) A quick win for White looks unlikely, but there is no resisting the power of a double check: **1 ♕d8+! ♔xd8 2 ♗b6++ ♔e8** (2...♔c8 is also met by 3 ♖d8#) **3 ♖d8#**.

12) A rook vs king line-up is often the trigger for a discovered check tactic: **1 ♘xe5!** (offering the queen, but the sacrifice is only temporary) **1...♗xd1** (1...fxe5 2 ♕xg4 wins a pawn and shatters Black's position) **2 ♘xc6+ ♔f7** (Black cannot prevent White from taking the queen with check) **3 ♘xd8+ ♖xd8 4 ♖xd1** and White has won a piece.

13) A typical tactic leads to mate by discovered check: **1 ♕xh7+! ♔xh7 2 ♖h3+ ♔g7 3 ♗h6+ ♔h7 4 ♗f8#**.

14) White uses a double check to force a 'semi-smothered' mate: **1 ♘f7+ ♔e8 2 ♘d6++ ♔d8** (2...♔f8 is met by 3 ♕f7# or 3 ♗h6#) **3 ♕e8+! ♘xe8** (or 3...♔c7 4 ♕xc8#) **4 ♘f7#**. The king's one possible flight-square on c7 is covered by the white bishop.

15) Black must act quickly as White threatens to mate by ♕xf7+. The correct sequence forces mate by a series of checks: **1...♖c1++! 2 ♔xc1 ♕h1+ 3 ♔d2 ♕d1+ 4 ♔e3** (or 4 ♔c3 ♕d3#) **4...♕d3#**.

16) **1 ♖b8!** (pinning the queen, but not 1 ♘f6+? ♔g7 2 ♖g2+ ♔h6, when White has no follow-up) **1...♕xb8** (now the queen is vulnerable to a possible discovered check) **2 ♘f6+ ♔g7** (2...♔h8 3 ♘d7+ is the same) **3 ♘d7+** and the queen falls, leaving White two pieces ahead.

63

17) A 'staircase' sequence of double checks chases White's king to its doom: **1...♕xg2+! 2 ♔xg2 ♖g3++ 3 ♔h2 ♖g2++ 4 ♔h1 ♖h2++ 5 ♔g1 ♖h1#**.

18) Black conjures a spectacular finish: **1...♕xh2+!** (not 1...f1♕+?? 2 ♖xf1+, when there is no mate on h2 because Black is in check, the sort of thing that's easy to overlook in a game) **2 ♔xh2 f1♘++!** (it's important to give the more dangerous double check rather than a simple discovered check, so that White is forced to move his king; here 2...f1♕+? 3 ♕xd2 leads nowhere) **3 ♔h3** (or 3 ♔h1 ♖h2#) **3...♖h2#**.

19) White wins with a typical kingside breakthrough: **1 ♗xh6! gxh6 2 ♕xh6+ ♔g8** (now the other bishop joins the attack) **3 ♗h7+ ♔h8 4 ♗g6+** (this discovered check leads to a quick mate) **4...♔g8 5 ♕h7+ ♔f8 6 ♕xf7#**.

20) A preliminary sacrifice opens the diagonal from b3 to g8 for a discovered check: **1 ♘e6!** (forking the rooks, so Black must take) **1...fxe6 2 dxe6 ♕e8** (there is nothing better) **3 e7+ ♔h8** and now taking either rook leaves White rook for knight up.

21) White's queen is attacked, but that doesn't matter if he gives a double check, since such a check can only be met by a king move : **1 ♗xg7++! ♔xg7 2 ♕h7+ ♔f6** (2...♔f8 3 ♕f7#) **3 ♕f7+ ♔g5 4 h4+ ♔h6 5 ♕h7#**.

22) White won with a beautiful and unusual combination: **1 f7+!** (the first step is to draw Black's king onto the same file as the f1-rook; 1 ♖xc6? allows 1...♖hf3+! with *perpetual check* along the third rank) **1...♔xf7** (1...♔f8 2 ♖f6+ is a devastating discovered check) **2 ♖xc6!** (the second step is to deflect one black rook away with a sacrifice, leaving the other rook undefended) **2...♖xc6** (2...♖hf3+ 3 ♔g2 and 2...♖cf3+ 3 ♔e2! also leave White a piece up) **3 ♔g2+** followed by **4 ♔xh3** and White ends up a piece ahead. It's rare for the king to deliver discovered check, but here it's just what White needed to make his tactic work.

23) White's queen is under attack, so he needs a double check to have any impact. By sacrificing his bishop he can draw the enemy king into the correct position: **1 ♗g7+! ♔xg7 2 ♘e8++** (2 ♘xh5++? ♔h6 3 ♕g7+ ♔xh5 loses the knight and is much less clear) **2...♔h6** (or else it's immediate mate by ♕g7#) **3 ♕g7+ ♔g5** and now White has various ways to mate, the quickest being **4 h4+ ♔g4 5 ♗e2#**.

24) **1 ♘xe6+! fxe6** (1...♔e7 2 ♘e4+ gives White a crushing attack; for example, 2...♔xe6 3 ♘c5# or 2...f6 3 exf6+ ♔xe6 4 ♘c5+ ♔f7 5 fxg7+ ♔e8 6 ♕e2+ ♔f7 7 ♕e7#) **2 ♘e4+** (this is the only discovered check to win, emphasizing the point that the choice of which check to give is often very important) **2...♔e8 3 ♘d6+** (White chose ♘e4+ last move because it is the only way the knight can reach d6) **3...♔d7 4 ♕f7#**.

25) White crashes through with a sequences of sacrifices: **1 ♗xh7+! ♔xh7 2 ♕h5+ ♔g8 3 ♕h8+!** (this is the tough move to foresee, decoying the black king into position for a double check) **3...♔xh8 4 ♘g6++ ♔g8 5 ♖h8#**.

26) The rook on h1 currently has no moves, but its power can be unleashed to deadly effect by the correct sequences of sacrifices: **1 ♖g3+! fxg3 2 ♗xh7+! ♔xh7 3 hxg3+ ♔g8** and now **4 ♕h8#** is one possible mate.

27) The attack on g2 provides Black with a decisive tactic: **1...♖xg2! 2 ♖xe8** (after 2 ♖xg2 ♖xe2 3 d7 ♖xg2 4 d8♕ ♖d2+ the discovered check leaves Black with a decisive material advantage) **2...♖g6+** (2...♖g5+ and 2...♖g4+ are equally good, but 2...♖xf2+? 3 ♔g1

♖g2+? 4 ♔f1 lets White escape) **3 ♖g2 ♗xg2+** (3...♖xg2? 4 ♖c8! is another false path) **4 ♔g1 ♗c6+** (again the discovered check is crushing) followed by **5...♗xe8**. Black ends up with an extra rook.

28) Black wins with the famous 'see-saw' combination. After **1...♕xg2+! 2 ♘xg2 ♖xg2+ 3 ♔h1** Black could win the white queen by 3...♖g4+?, but this would still leave him a piece down. However, he can gobble up virtually all White's other pieces first by a back-and-forth manoeuvre: **3...♖xf2+! 4 ♔g1 ♖g2+ 5 ♔h1 ♖xc2+** (there's nothing White can do but watch helplessly while Black takes one thing after another) **6 ♔g1 ♖g2+ 7 ♔h1 ♖xb2+ 8 ♔g1 ♖g2+ 9 ♔h1 ♖xa2+ 10 ♔g1 ♖g2+ 11 ♔h1 ♖g4+** (the second rank has been cleared and now it's time to grab the queen) **12 ♔h2 ♖xh4+** and Black has an easy win with his three extra pawns.

29) Black's king is lacking defenders and White can break through by **1 ♕a6+ ♔a8 2 ♕xa7+! ♔xa7 3 ♖a1+ ♔b7 4 ♗a6+ ♔a7 5 ♗c8#** with mate by discovered check. This is a refined version of the mate from Exercise 13.

30) If the white rook were not pinned, he could mate at once by the double check ♖xe8#. By offering his queen, White can release the rook: **1 ♕g3!!** (1 ♔h1?? also unpins the rook, but allows mate in two by 1...♕xh6+) **1...♕xh6+** (the only way to avoid an immediate loss; if 1...♗xg3, then 2 ♖xe8#) **2 ♕h3 ♕d6** (2...♕xh3+ 3 ♔xh3 also loses since the bishop on e8 is attacked; Black cannot both save the bishop and avoid mate) **3 ♔h1** and now this wins as Black has no useful check so White either mates or wins a large amount of material.

31) 1 ♗c2+! (the only good square, blocking the b2-rook's path along White's second rank) **1...♔g8 2 ♖g2#**.

32) 1 ♕a8+ ♘b8 2 ♕xb7+ ♔d8! (2...♔xb7?? 3 ♗xd7# is indeed the same as in Exercise 9, but here Black can run away) **3 ♕xb8+ ♔e7** with a win for Black, as he is both attacking the white queen and threatening mate by ...♕xg2#.

33) After **1...♗g4!** (the only move to avoid disaster, and a good one; by attacking the queen, Black takes the sting out of White's discovered check) **2 ♕xg4 ♔xh7** Black is a piece for a pawn up and has a big advantage. If your opponent is threatening a discovered check, attacking the rear piece is often a good way to neutralize the threat (this doesn't work if the threat is a **double** check).

34) Playing for a discovered check is the correct course: **1 ♖f7+!** (1 ♖e8+? ♔g7 2 ♖g8+ ♔f6! 3 ♖xg1 wins the queen but stalemates Black) **1...♔g8 2 ♖f1+** and White grabs the queen without allowing stalemate.

35) The key moment arises after **1...♕xg2+!** (this is still the best move, even though it doesn't win) **2 ♘xg2 ♖xg2+ 3 ♔h1 ♖xf2+ 4 ♔g1 ♖g2+ 5 ♔h1**. Black should now force a draw by **5...♖f2+** or play **5...♖g4+ 6 ♔h2 ♖xh4+** with an equal ending. Playing as in Exercise 28 loses: **5...♖xc2+? 6 ♖f3! ♗xf3+ 7 ♔g1 ♖g2+ 8 ♔f1** and the white king slips out of the 'see-saw', securing him a decisive material advantage.

36) This is a little similar to Exercise 33 but requires a different approach. 1...g6? is tempting, but loses to the beautiful 2 ♗xg6+ ♔g7 3 ♕h7+ ♔f6 4 ♗f7!! (threatening 5 ♕g6# and 5 ♘d5+ ♔g5 6 ♕h5#) 4...e4 (4...♖xf7 5 ♕h6#) 5 ♘d5+ ♔e5 6 ♕g7+ ♗f6 7 ♕g3+ with a quick mate. The solution is **1...♗g5!**, so that the discovered check **2 ♗g6+** (2 ♗xf5+ ♗h6 is the same) is met by **2...♗h6** and the attack is dead, leaving Black a piece up.

7 Removing the Guard

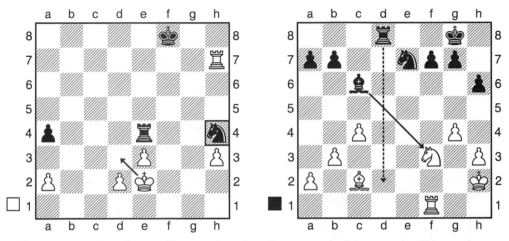

If one enemy piece is guarding another, then the removal of the guard will leave the second piece with one defender less and it may then be vulnerable to capture. There are generally two ways the guard can be eliminated. The first is that the defending piece can be attacked and chased away, as in the left-hand diagram above. Black's rook is guarding the attacked knight on h4 and if it can be driven off the fourth rank then the knight can be captured. Although it sounds simple, White has to take care not to allow Black to escape by giving a check. For example, 1 d3? ♖b4 2 a3 is wrong as Black plays 2...♖b2+ and then moves the attacked knight. The correct sequence is **1 ♔d3 ♖b4 2 ♔c3** (again 2 a3? ♖b3+ 3 ♔e4 ♘g6 lets Black off the hook) **2...♖e4 3 d3** and now there are no safe squares left for the rook on the fourth rank. After **3...♖xe3 4 ♖xh4** White can win with his two extra pawns.

Another way to remove the guard is by exchanging the defending piece. In the right-hand diagram above, White's knight on f3 is not defending another white piece. However, it is covering the crucial square d2 and so preventing a fork by ...♖d2+. Exchanging the knight leaves d2 undefended, so Black can win a piece with **1...♗xf3 2 ♖xf3 ♖d2+** followed by ...♖xc2.

Here are some tips for solving the exercises:

- Look for enemy pieces that guard one another, and see if one can be exchanged.
- The idea of removing the guard is often combined with other tactics, especially forks (as in the second position above), so if an enemy piece is preventing a fork, look to see if it can be eliminated.
- If the piece you are chasing away can move so as to create a threat, then the removing the guard tactic may not work, so you must take care to check for this possibility.

Exercises

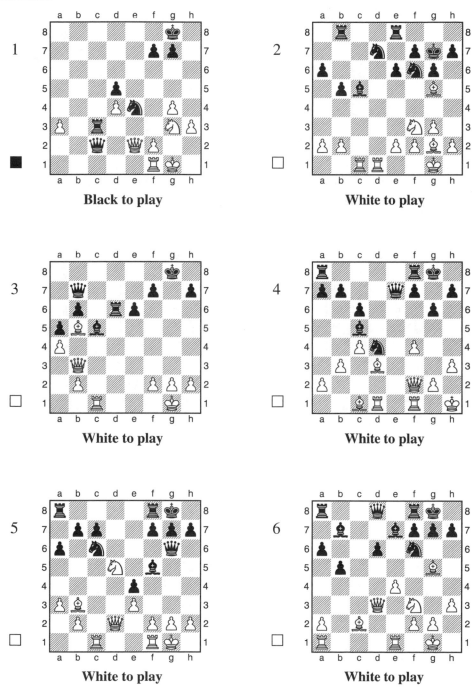

1 **Black to play**

2 **White to play**

3 **White to play**

4 **White to play**

5 **White to play**

6 **White to play**

Tougher Positions

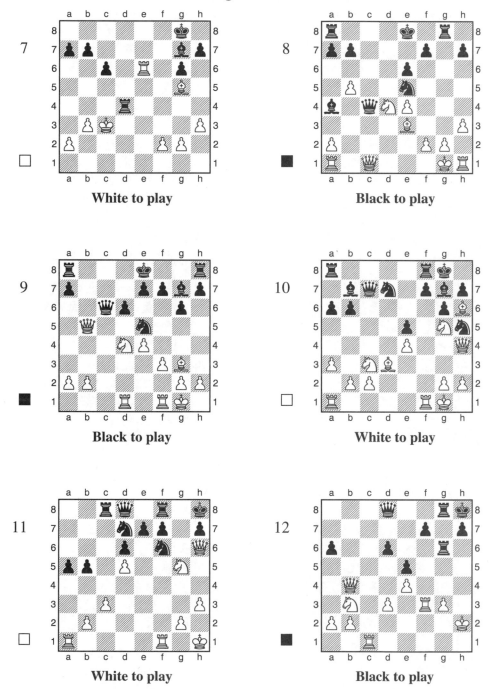

7 — White to play

8 — Black to play

9 — Black to play

10 — White to play

11 — White to play

12 — Black to play

Does the Tactic Work?

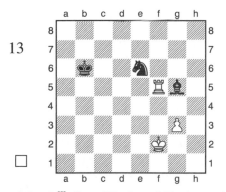

13

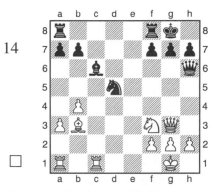

14

After **1 ♖e5** can Black avoid losing a piece and the game?

How can Black meet **1 b5**?

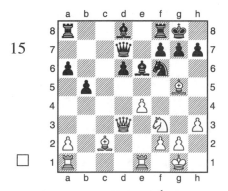

15

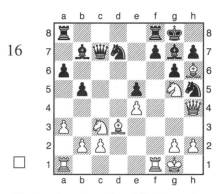

16

Can Black defend after **1 ♗xf6**, intending **1...♗xf6 2 e5**?

First solve Exercise 10. Does the same idea win here?

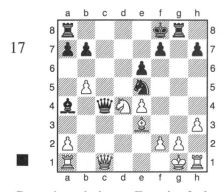

17

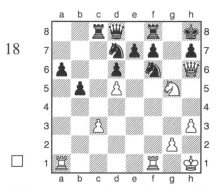

18

Does the solution to Exercise 8 also win in this position?

This is very similar to Exercise 11. Can White win the same way?

Solutions to Removing the Guard Exercises

1) The knight is the only piece defending the white queen, and Black can eliminate it with check: **1...♖xg3+! 2 fxg3 ♕xe2** and Black wins.

2) Black has a chain of defenders: the f6-knight defends the d7-knight, which in turn defends the c5-bishop. The capture **1 ♗xf6+** breaks the chain and Black loses a piece after **1...♘xf6 2 ♖xc5** or **1...♔xf6 2 ♖xd7**.

3) Removing the c5-bishop sets up a decisive fork: **1 ♖xc5!** (not 1 ♕g3+? ♔f8 2 ♖xc5? as then 2...♖d1+ 3 ♗f1 bxc5 wins for Black) **1...bxc5** (here 1...♖d1+ loses to 2 ♕xd1) **2 ♕g3+** followed by **3 ♕xd6**, with an extra piece for White.

4) The c5-bishop is tied to the defence of the knight on d4. **1 b4 ♗b6** (1...♗xb4 2 ♕xd4 also costs Black a piece) **2 c5** chases the defending bishop away and wins a piece.

5) Eliminating the c6-knight leads to a crushing knight fork: **1 ♖xc6! bxc6** (or 1...♕xc6 2 ♘e7+) **2 ♘e7+ ♔h8 3 ♘xg6+** wins the enemy queen.

6) White would like to play e5, opening a line for a possible mate on h7, but the f6-knight is covering the mate, so it must first be eliminated: **1 ♗xf6** (it's important to get the order of moves right, since 1 e5? dxe5 2 ♗xf6 fails due to 2...♕xd3) **1...♗xf6** (1...gxf6 2 e5 is no better as Black cannot defend h7 and 2...♖e8 3 ♕xh7+ ♔f8 4 ♕h8# only delays the end) **2 e5** and White wins a piece as he threatens both 3 ♕xh7# and 3 exf6.

7) Black is threatening to give a discovered check, but it is White's move and he can win by removing the guard of the d4-rook: **1 ♖e8+ ♔f7 2 ♖e7+ ♔f8 3 ♖xg7!** and White wins a piece.

8) Black can win by destroying the d4-knight's guard of f3 with a spectacular sacrifice: **1...♕xd4! 2 ♗xd4 ♘f3+ 3 ♔f1 ♗xb5+** and mate next move.

9) First Black opens the line from g7 to d4 and then eliminates the knight defending the white queen: **1...♘xf3+! 2 gxf3** (after 2 ♔h1 ♘xd4 Black wins a piece, while 2 ♖xf3 ♗xd4+ and 2 ♘xf3 ♕xb5 both cost White his queen) **2...♗xd4+** followed by **3...♕xb5** and Black wins.

10) **1 ♗xg7 ♔xg7** (1...♕c5+ 2 ♔h1 ♔xg7 also loses to 3 ♖xf7+! ♖xf7 4 ♘e6+, since from e6 the knight attacks c5 as well as c7) **2 ♖xf7+!** (White cannot play ♘e6+ at once as Black's pawn is guarding that square, but a preliminary sacrifice destroys Black's defence) **2...♖xf7 3 ♘e6+** and White wins the queen.

11) The defensive chain d7-f6-h7 can be destroyed by repeated sacrifices on the same square: **1 ♖xf6! ♘xf6 2 ♖f1** and there's no defence to the threat of **3 ♖xf6** followed by mate on h7. Note that 2...♖g8 allows mate by 3 ♘xf7#.

12) If the black queen could enter the attack then White would be finished, but h4 is guarded by a white pawn. A rook sacrifice removes this guard and wins: **1...♖xg3! 2 ♖xg3 ♕h4+ 3 ♔g2 ♕xg3+** (3...♖xg3+ also leads to mate) **4 ♔f1 ♕g1+ 5 ♔e2 ♖g2+ 6 ♔f3 ♕f2#**. Sacrifices such as these, which demolish the defences to the opponent's king, are often based on the theme of removing the guard.

13) After **1 ♖e5** Black can save himself by the fork **1...♘c5! 2 ♖xg5 ♘e4+**, leading to a draw.

14) **1 b5** can be answered by **1...♘f4!**, which gains time as White must deal with the possibility of ...♘e2+. After **2 ♗c4 ♗d5** the position is balanced.

15) Here **1 ♗xf6?** (1 ♖ad1 is better) is well answered by **1...♗c4!**, forcing the white queen off the d3-h7 diagonal, after which Black can safely play 2...♗xf6.

16) The small difference from Exercise 10 (black pawn on b5 rather than b6) allows Black to avoid defeat. The point is that **1 ♗xg7 ♛b6+!** enables Black to remove his queen from the exposed square c7 with gain of time, and after **2 ♔h1 ♔xg7** the position is equal, since the ♖xf7+ and ♘e6+ tactic no longer works.

17) The position of the king on f8 (rather than e8, as in Exercise 8) means that **1...♛xd4??** is actually a blunder. After **2 ♛a3+! ♔e8 3 ♗xd4** the white queen stops the check on f3 and White is simply a queen up. When you play a tactic, it's important to make sure that your opponent doesn't have a check or other disrupting move that causes your tactic to misfire. **Every position is different**, and even the most familiar ideas will fail in certain situations.

18) The difference in the position of the queenside pawns compared to Exercise 11 means that Black has a saving resource: **1 ♖xf6 ♘xf6 2 ♖f1 ♛a5!** (the only move, as otherwise 3 ♖xf6 does indeed win) **3 ♖xf6 ♛a1+ 4 ♔h2 ♛b1** and Black just manages to cover h7 and prevent the mate. After **5 ♘xf7+ ♖xf7 6 ♖xf7 ♛g6** the position is equal.

REMOVING THE GUARD

8 In-Between Moves

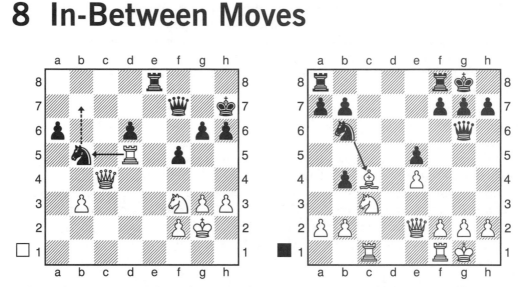

An *in-between move* is one that occurs between two moves which are normally played one after the other. Typically, one player makes a capture, expecting an immediate recapture. Instead, his opponent plays a different move, creating a strong threat, and only makes the recapture on the following move. This additional move comes 'in-between' the capture and the recapture, hence the name. This may sound a bit abstract, but the left-hand diagram should make the idea clear. White plays **1 ♖xb5!**, attacking the black queen. At first sight this is a blunder, because after 1...♕xc4 2 bxc4 axb5 White has lost rook for knight. This is where the in-between move comes in. After **1...♕xc4** White instead plays **2 ♖b7+** and only recaptures the queen on the following move. The result is that White wins a piece.

The in-between move is often a check, as above, but it doesn't have to be. However, it must create a strong threat, because the initial capture puts the opponent ahead on material. In the right-hand diagram above, White is temporarily a piece up, and Black should simply regain the piece by playing 1...bxc3. However, he might be tempted to play **1...♘xc4?**, anticipating that after 2 ♕xc4? he can then take on c3. However, White instead plays the in-between move **2 ♘d5!**, which removes the knight from attack and at the same time creates the powerful threat of ♘e7+. This threat cannot be ignored, so Black has no time to move the attacked knight. After, for example, **2...♔h8** (moving the queen doesn't help) White continues **3 ♖xc4** or **3 ♕xc4** with an extra piece.

Here are some tips for solving the exercises:

- In many exercises there is a sequences of captures, and you must choose the correct moment to insert the in-between move.
- In-between moves are often combined with a discovered attack. Exercise 4 is one example, but there are others.
- In the endgame, a check is sometimes useful as an in-between move to force the enemy king to an inferior position. Exercise 20 is one example.

Exercises

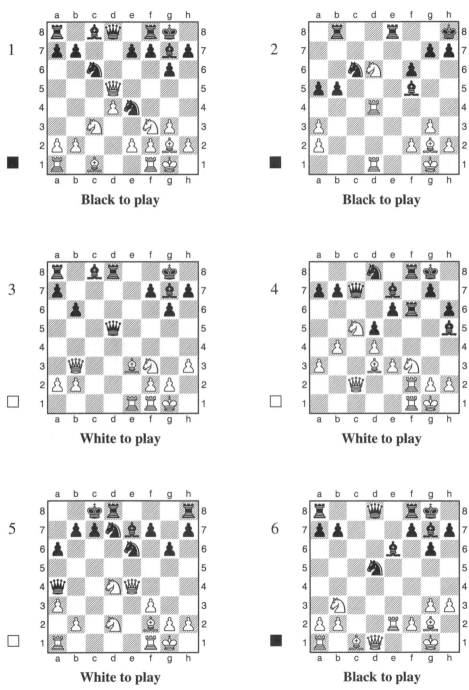

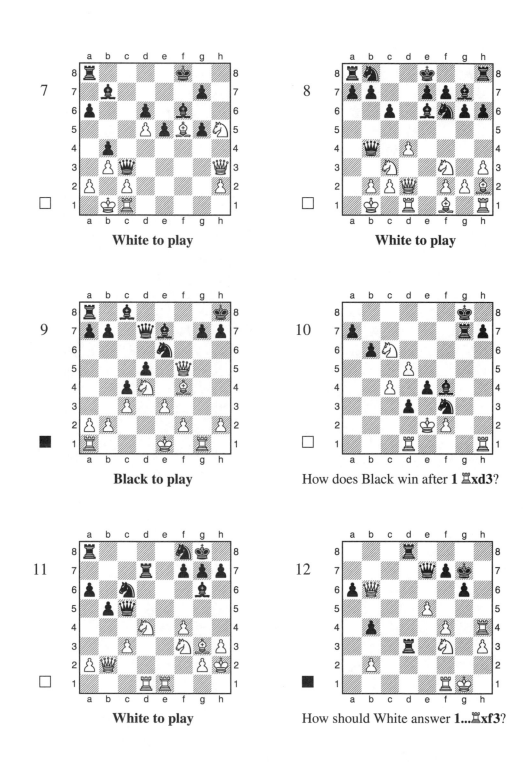

7 White to play

8 White to play

9 Black to play

10 How does Black win after **1 ♖xd3**?

11 White to play

12 How should White answer **1...♖xf3**?

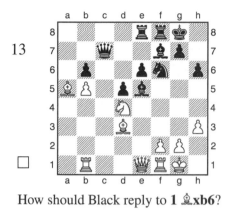

13

How should Black reply to **1 &xb6**?

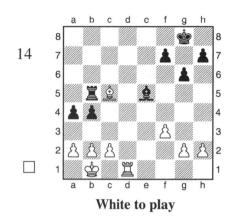

14

White to play

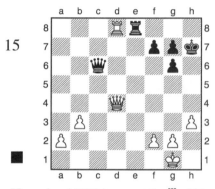

15

How should White meet **1...&xd8**?

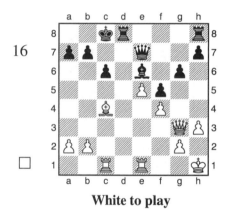

16

White to play

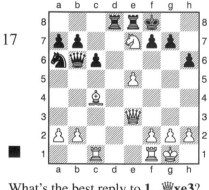

17

What's the best reply to **1...&xe3**?

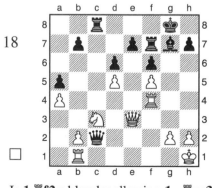

18

Is **1 &f2** a blunder allowing **1...&xc3**?

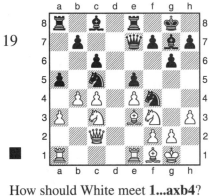

19

How should White meet **1...axb4**?

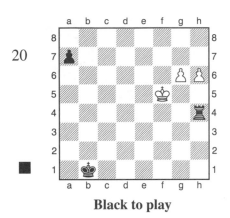

20

Black to play

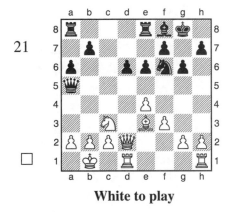

21

White to play

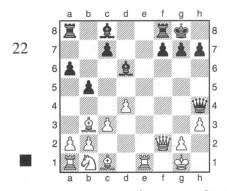

22

Which is better, **1...♗g3** or **1...♗h2+ 2 ♔f1 ♗g3**?

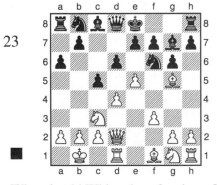

23

What should White play after **1...cxd4**?

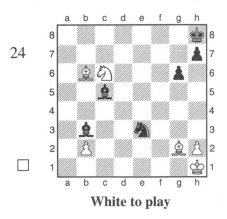

24

White to play

25

White to play

26

White to play

27

Black to play

28

What is the best reply to **1...♘g4**?

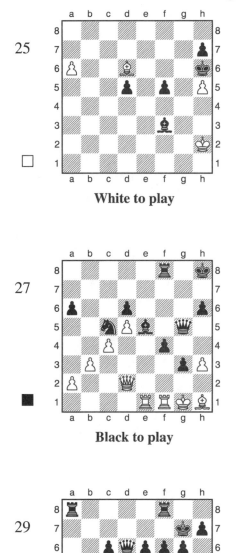

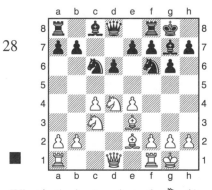

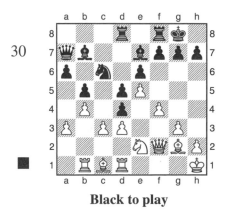

29

White to play

30

Black to play

Does the Tactic Work?

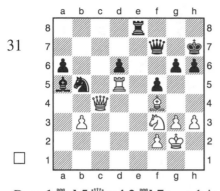

31

Does **1 ♖xb5 ♕xc4 2 ♖b7+** work in this position?

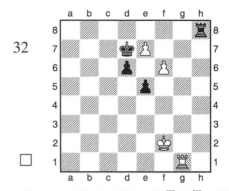

32

Why does the 'brilliant' **1 ♖g8 ♖xg8 2 f7** rebound on White?

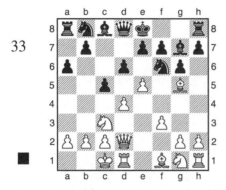

33

Does **1...cxd4** lose as in Exercise 23?

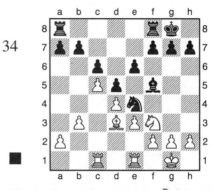

34

Black played the tricky **1...♘d6**. What is the best reply?

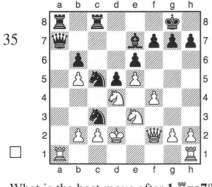

35

What is the best move after **1 ♖xa7**?

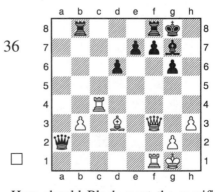

36

How should Black meet the sacrifice **1 ♗xg6**?

Solutions to In-Between Moves Exercises

1) **1...♘xc3!** (now White's queen is undefended, so he must take on d8) **2 ♕xd8 ♘xe2+** followed by **3...♖xd8** and Black wins a piece.

2) Black can win material by **1...♘xd4! 2 ♘xe8** (2 ♖xd4 ♖e1+ 3 ♗f1 ♗h3 leads to a quick mate) and now the in-between move **2...♘e2+** wins a piece after **3 ♔f1 ♖xe8**.

3) This is a typical tactic involving a combination of skewer and in-between move: **1 ♖d1! ♕xb3 2 ♖xd8+ ♗f8 3 axb3** and White wins a rook.

4) The discovered attack plus in-between move idea has claimed countless victims. Here **1 ♘e4!** attacks the undefended black queen and after **1...♕xc2 2 ♘xf6+ gxf6 3 ♖xc2** White is rook for bishop up.

5) The discovered attack and in-between move tactic strikes yet again: **1 ♘f5! ♕xe4 2 ♘xe7+ ♔b8 3 ♘xe4** and White has won a piece.

6) Black can win material by **1...♘c3!** (not 1...♘f4?? 2 ♗xf4, defending the white queen) attacking the undefended white queen and the rook on e2. After **2 ♕xd8** the in-between check **2...♘xe2+** leads to an easy win: **3 ♔f1 ♖axd8 4 ♔xe2 ♗c4+** with extra material and a crushing attack.

7) A simple in-between move nets a piece: **1 ♘xf6! ♕xh3** (or 1...gxf6 2 ♕h8+ ♔f7 3 ♕h7+ ♔e8 4 ♕d7+ ♔f8 5 ♗e6 followed by mate) **2 ♘d7+** (the knight moves to safety with gain of time, but not 2 ♘h7+?, which allows 2...♕xh7 and Black escapes) **2...♔e7 3 ♗xh3**.

8) **1 ♘b5!** (threatening both 2 ♕xb4 and 2 ♘c7+, so Black must take the queen) **1...♕xd2 2 ♘c7+** (the crucial in-between check) **2...♔d7 3 ♖xd2** (3 ♘xd2 is also good) and the transfer of the knight to c7 has trapped the rook on a8, so White will win rook for knight.

9) The win involves two in-between checks: **1...♘xd4! 2 ♕xd7 ♘f3+ 3 ♔e2** (3 ♔f1 ♗xd7 may be relatively best, but still leaves Black with a bishop and a knight for a rook) **3...♘xg1+ 4 ♖xg1 ♗xd7** with an extra piece for Black.

10) **1 ♖xd3** is met by **1...♘g1+!** (1...exd3+? 2 ♔xf3 is only equal) **2 ♖xg1 exd3+** (the second in-between move is decisive) **3 ♔f1 ♖xg1+ 4 ♔xg1 d2** and the pawn promotes.

11) White wins material with two in-between moves: **1 ♘xc6! ♖xd1** (after 1...♕xc6 the fork 2 ♘e5 wins) **2 ♘e7+** (the first in-between move, but not 2 ♖xd1? ♕xc6 and Black is safe) **2...♔h8 3 ♘xg6+** (the second in-between move; 3 ♖xd1? ♕xe7 is inferior and allows Black to escape) **3...hxg6 4 ♖xd1** and White is a piece ahead.

12) **1...♖xf3** is met by **2 ♕f6+!** (Black was hoping for 2 ♗xf3? ♕xh4, but an in-between finesse destroys his hopes) **2...♕xf6 3 exf6+** followed by **4 ♗xf3**, with an extra rook for White.

13) **1 ♗xb6??** is actually a blunder. The idea is 1...♕xb6? 2 ♕xe5, but after **1...♗h2+! 2 ♔h1 ♕xb6** Black stays a piece up, since 3 ♔xh2 ♕xd4 does not help White.

14) **1 ♖d8+!** (the immediate 1 ♖d5? ♗c7 just leaves White in an awkward pin, but this in-between check drives Black's king to an inferior square) **1...♔g7 2 ♖d5** (now this wins, as White threatens both 3 ♖xe5 and 3 ♗f8+ with a discovered attack) **2...♗d6** (trying to prevent ♗f8+, but allowing a different check) **3 ♗d4+** and White wins a rook.

15) After **1...♖xd8?** (1...♕c1+! 2 ♔h2 ♖xd8 is better, since then 3 ♕h4+ ♕h6! 4 ♕xd8 ♕f4+ really does draw) the immediate recapture 2 ♕xd8? allows Black to play 2...♕c1+ 3 ♔h2 ♕f4+ with a draw by *perpetual check* (see Chapter 12). Instead the in-between check **2**

♕h4+! leads to the capture of the black rook with check, and after **2...♔g8 3 ♕xd8+ ♔h7 4 ♕d2** White is a safe two pawns ahead.

16) A surprising move gains material for White: **1 ♕a3!** (attacking the enemy queen; 1 ♕g5? ♖he8 is ineffective) **1...♖he8** (1...♕xa3 2 ♗xe6+ costs Black a piece) **2 ♕xa7** and White has won an important pawn.

17) Black's **1...♕xe3?** intends 2 fxe3? ♖xe7, which is safe enough for Black. However, the in-between check **2 ♘g6+!** is decisive since **2...fxg6 3 fxe3+ ♔e7 4 ♖f7#** is mate while **2...♔g8 3 fxe3** leaves White a piece ahead.

18) **1 ♖f2** is not a mistake as **1...♖xc3?** is met by the in-between move **2 ♕e1!**, defending the b1-rook and leaving Black's queen under attack. The queen must move, but then White can safely take on c3. After **2...♕xa4 3 bxc3** White is material up with a winning position.

19) After Black's **1...axb4?**, the obvious 2 axb4? ♘a6 leads to no great advantage for White. When your opponent takes something, there's a natural instinct to take back automatically, but it's worth looking to see if there's an alternative. Here White can insert **2 ♗xc5!** **♕xc5** before taking back with **3 axb4**. Then Black's queen and rook are both under attack and White wins material.

20) A cunning in-between check enables Black to give up his rook for the two white pawns, after which the a-pawn cannot be stopped: **1...♖h5+!** (1...♖xh6? 2 g7 even wins for White as the pawn promotes after 2...♖h5+ 3 ♔f4 ♖h4+ 4 ♔f3 ♖h3+ 5 ♔g2) **2 ♔f6** (or 2 ♔f4 ♖xh6 3 g7 ♖g6) **2...♖xh6** (now the g-pawn is pinned) **3 ♔f7 ♖xg6 4 ♔xg6 a5** and Black wins.

21) **1 ♘d5!** (attacking the queen on a5 and the knight on f6) **1...♕xd2** (after 1...♕d8 2 ♗b6 the queen must abandon the knight on f6) **2 ♘xf6+** (the first in-between move) **2...♔g7 3 ♘xe8+** (the second in-between move decides the game; not 3 ♖xd2? ♔xf6 and Black escapes) **3...♖xe8 4 ♖xd2** and White has won a rook.

22) The in-between check is essential. 1...♗g3?? is a serious blunder due to 2 ♕xf7+! ♖xf7 3 ♖e8#, but **1...♖h2+! 2 ♔f1 ♗g3** is possible, with chances for both sides. Here 3 ♕xf7+?? fails because the reply **3...♖xf7+** is check and so White cannot mate.

23) Sometimes there's a whole chain of in-between moves. Here **1...cxd4?** loses to **2 exf6! dxc3** (or else White remains a piece up, for example after 2...exf6 3 ♕xd4 fxg5 4 ♕xg7) **3 fxg7 cxd2 4 gxh8♕+** and White wins a rook and a piece.

24) An in-between move decides the game: **1 ♗xc5 ♘xg2 2 ♘e7!** (Black's idea is 2 ♔xg2? ♗d5+ followed by ...♗xc6, but by threatening 3 ♗d4# White saves his knight with gain of time) **2...♔g7 3 ♔xg2** and White has won a piece.

25) White would like to bring his bishop to d4, blocking the d5-pawn, and then play a7, but this only works if White can gain time. The correct sequence is **1 ♔g3!** (first White hits the bishop) **1...♗h1 2 ♗h4!** (and then he threatens ♗f8#, forcing the enemy king to move) **2...♔g7 3 ♗e5+** (thanks to the two in-between moves, White gets his bishop to d4 without allowing ...d4 by Black) **3...♔f7 4 ♗d4** followed by **5 a7**, winning.

26) This is a typical tactic with a small twist: **1 ♗xf7+! ♔xf7 2 ♘g5+** (if Black moves his king, then White replies 3 ♕xg4 with an extra pawn) **2...♗xg5** (normally this would be a good reply, but here an in-between discovered check allows White to take two black pieces in a row) **3 fxg5+** followed by **4 ♕xg4** and again White has won an important pawn.

27) **1...f3!** (threatening both 2...f2+ and 2...♕xd2) **2 ♕xg5 f2+** (the first in-between check) **3 ♔g2** (or 3 ♖xf2 gxf2+ 4 ♔f1 fxe1♕++ 5 ♔xe1 hxg5 and Black wins) **3...fxe1♘+!** (it is essential that this is check; 3...fxe1♕?? loses to 4 ♕xh6+ ♔g8 5 ♖xf8#) **4 ♖xe1 hxg5** and Black has won a piece.

28) **1...♘g4?** falls into an opening trap that costs Black a piece. Hundreds of players have made this same mistake, so it's well worth knowing! **2 ♗xg4!** (2 ♘xc6? ♘xe3 is fine for Black) **2...♗xg4** (2...♘xd4 3 ♗xc8! also costs Black a piece) **3 ♘xc6!** (this in-between move is the point) **3...♗xd1** (or 3...bxc6 4 ♕xg4) **4 ♘xd8 ♖fxd8 5 ♖fxd1** and White is a safe piece ahead.

29) **1 ♕a3!** (the attacked bishop is almost trapped and has only one safe square) **1...♗b5 2 ♖xb5!** (a typical in-between move tactic similar to the first example at the start of the chapter) **2...♕xa3 3 ♖b7+ ♔f7 4 ♖xf7+ ♔xf7 5 bxa3** and White has won a piece.

30) Black wins with a surprising in-between tactic based on pawn promotion: **1...dxc3! 2 ♕xa7 c2!** (instead of recapturing the queen immediately, Black threatens to promote on b1 or d1) **3 ♗e3** (3 ♕g1 cxb1♕ is even worse) **3...cxd1♕+ 4 ♖xd1 ♘xa7 5 ♗xa7 ♖c8** and Black has a rook-for-knight advantage.

31) The tactical idea **1 ♖xb5? ♕xc4 2 ♖b7+** doesn't work in this position. Black can reply **2...♔c7! 3 ♖xc7+ ♗xc7** with a winning material advantage.

32) The tactic **1 ♖g8? ♖xg8 2 f7** may appear to promote a pawn, but the counter-sacrifice **2...♖g2+!** (not 2...♔xe7? 3 fxg8♕) deprives White of the possibility of promoting on g8 and leads to a win for Black after **3 ♔xg2 ♔xe7**.

33) Here **1...cxd4!** is possible because there is a crucial difference. The white king is on c1 rather than b1, so when Black takes on d2 it is check: **2 exf6 dxc3 3 fxg7??** (3 ♕e3 is better, with a wild but roughly balanced position) **3...cxd2+** followed by ...♖g8 and Black wins.

34) After **1...♘d6?** both 2 cxd6? ♗xd3 3 ♘e5 ♗g6 and 2 ♗xf5? ♘xf5 lead to equality, but the astonishing in-between move **2 ♗a6!!** gives White a large advantage. Black has nothing better than **2...bxa6** (after 2...♘e4 3 ♗xb7 White wins two pawns) **3 cxd6** (compared to 2 cxd6? ♗xd3, Black's c6-pawn is undefended and under attack from the rook on c1) **3...♖ac8 4 ♘e5**, but even here White will win a pawn with a very strong position.

35) After **1 ♖xa7**, 1...♖xa7? 2 ♕f3 ♘5e4+ 3 ♔d3 is roughly equal, while 1...♘3e4+? 2 ♔e2 ♘xf2 3 ♖xa8 (3 ♖ha1! is also strong) 3...♖xa8 4 ♔xf2 is good for White since he is pawn ahead. However, the in-between move **1...♘5e4+!** wins. Then **2 ♔e1** (2 ♔d3 ♘xf2+ and 2 ♔c1 ♖xa7 are also hopeless for White) **2...♖xa7!** (by threatening to mate with ...♖a1+, Black gives White no time to save his queen) **3 bxc3 ♘xf2 4 ♔xf2 ♖xc3** leaves Black well ahead on material.

36) After **1 ♗xg6?**, the obvious 1...fxg6? leads to a draw after 2 ♕d5+ ♔h8 (not 2...♔h7? 3 ♖h4+ ♗h6 4 ♖f7+ and White mates) 3 ♖h4+ ♗h6 4 ♖xh6+ ♔g7 5 ♖xg6+ ♔xg6 6 ♕e4+, with perpetual check from the queen. However, the in-between check **1...♕a7+!** refutes White's sacrifice. Then **2 ♔h1 fxg6 3 ♕d5+ e6 4 ♕xe6+ ♔h7** (4...♖f7 is also good) **5 ♖h4+ ♗h6** wins for Black because the queen on a7 covers f7 and so prevents ♖f7+. Checks make excellent in-between moves and it's always worth looking to see if there's one that changes the situation in your favour.

9 Trapped Piece

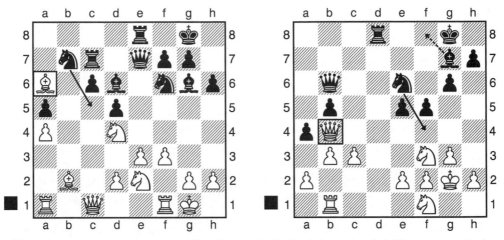

Trapping an enemy piece is an effective method of gaining material. The concept is simple enough: you attack an enemy piece that cannot move to a safe square and which cannot be adequately defended. The left-hand diagram above is an example. Black plays **1...♘c5**, which attacks the bishop on a6. Black can simply take it wherever it moves, and there is no way White can defend the bishop. Pieces which have ventured into enemy territory, as the bishop did here, are especially vulnerable to being trapped. You should be careful when sending a piece on an away mission amongst the opponent's forces, and make sure that it can return if necessary. This applies especially to the queen which, despite its great mobility, can easily find itself without a retreat.

If a piece is close to being trapped, then it may be possible to cut off the last escape route. In the right-hand diagram the white queen is short of squares and can be attacked by ...♗f8, but at the moment it can flee to h4. Chasing pieces around without a clear aim is generally not a good idea, but here Black has a trick that turns a near-miss into a direct hit. By playing the preliminary **1...♘f4+!**, Black seals the fourth rank and blocks the queen's path to safety. After **2 gxf4 ♗f8** the queen is trapped and Black wins it in return for a bishop and a knight, a large gain of material.

Here are some tips for solving the exercises:

• Look for enemy pieces that have few or no safe squares to move to.
• If there is currently an escape route, see if you can cut it off.
• Sometimes you can gain time by attacking one piece in order to trap another.

Exercises

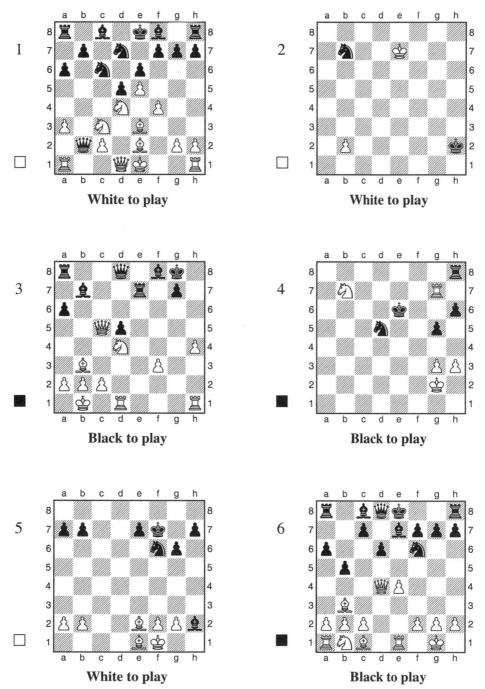

1 — White to play

2 — White to play

3 — Black to play

4 — Black to play

5 — White to play

6 — Black to play

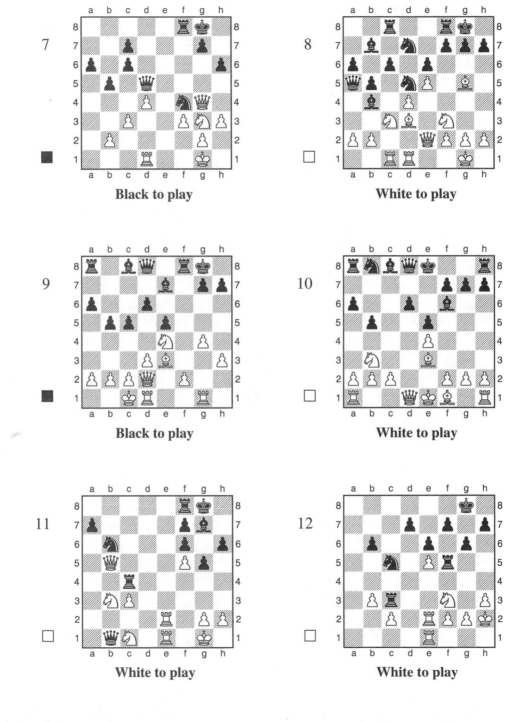

7 Black to play

8 White to play

9 Black to play

10 White to play

11 White to play

12 White to play

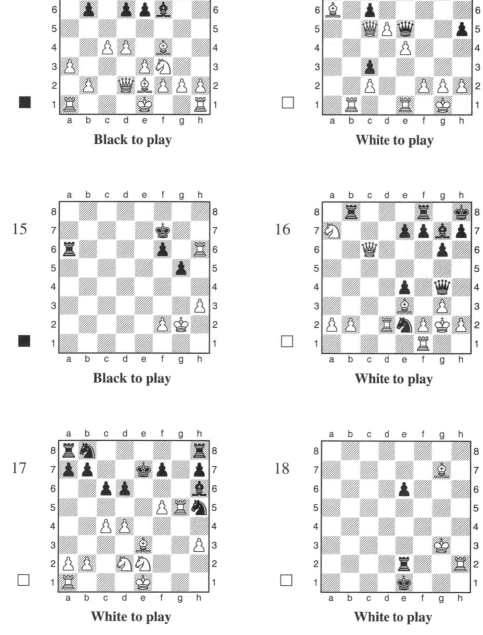

13 Black to play

14 White to play

15 Black to play

16 White to play

17 White to play

18 White to play

Tougher Positions

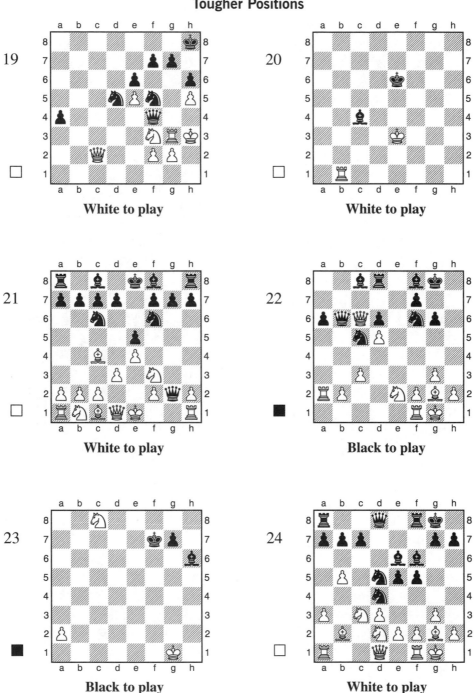

19 □ White to play

20 □ White to play

21 □ White to play

22 ■ Black to play

23 ■ Black to play

24 □ White to play

Does the Tactic Work?

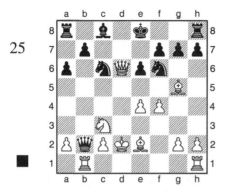

25

Can Black's queen be rescued without losing a piece?

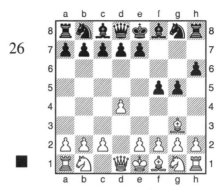

26

Does White lose his bishop after **1...f4**?

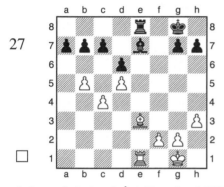

27

Is it good to play **1 ♗xa7** or should White be worried about **1...b6** followed by **2...♔f7** and **3...♖a8**?

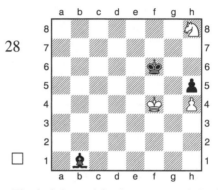

28

The knight on h8 seems trapped. Is there any way for White to save the game?

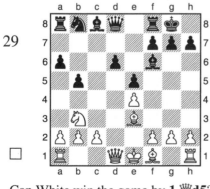

29

Can White win the game by **1 ♕d5**?

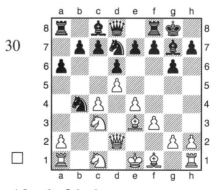

30

After **1 a3** is there any way to save the knight on b4?

Solutions to Trapped Piece Exercises

1) Black's queen has ventured too far into enemy territory and now pays the price: **1 ♘a4** and the queen is trapped.

2) After **1 b4!** there's no escape for the knight and White wins: **1...♔g3 2 ♔d7 ♔f4 3 ♔c7 ♔e5 4 ♔xb7** followed by promoting the pawn.

3) Any move by the e7-rook unveils a discovered attack on the white queen, but which square should the rook move to? The answer is e3 since **1...♖e3!** prevents ♕c3 and thereby traps the white queen. Not 1...♖c7? due to 2 ♕b6 or 2 ♕a5.

4) After **1...♘e7!** there's no defence to the threat of **2...♔f6**, trapping the rook.

5) Black's bishop has been too adventurous and after **1 g3** there is no way to meet the threat of **2 ♔g2**. This standard idea has occurred countless times and you should always take care when taking a pawn on a2 or h2 with a bishop (a7 or h7 if you are White), in case it gets trapped this way.

6) This is a trap that in various forms has caught out hundreds of players: **1...c5** (gaining time by attacking the queen) **2 ♕d1 c4** and now the bishop is lost.

7) Black wins by **1...h5 2 ♕h4** (2 ♘xh5 is relatively best, but still loses a piece) **2...g5**, trapping the queen.

8) In a surprising twist, White wins a piece with **1 ♘xd5 cxd5** (1...exd5 is also met by 2 a3) **2 a3 ♖xc1 3 ♖xc1** and the bishop on b4 is trapped.

9) **1...d5!** gains time and traps the bishop after **2 ♘g3 d4** or **2 ♘xc5 d4**.

10) Another typical opening trap results in the loss of Black's rook after **1 ♕d5**. Black can try to give up the rook and imprison the queen on a8 by **1...♗c7 2 ♕xa8 ♗b7** (2...♘c6 3 ♗b6! ♕d7 4 0-0-0 0-0 5 ♘c5 also frees the queen), but after **3 ♕a7 ♘c6 4 ♕b6** it slips out and White remains a rook ahead.

11) Black's queen gets caught by **1 ♘a2! ♕d3 2 ♖d2**.

12) White gains time by attacking one rook in order to trap the other: **1 ♘d4 ♖f4** (or any other square) **2 ♘b5** and White wins.

13) The g-pawn's advance wreaks havoc in White's position: **1...g5 2 ♗g3 g4 3 ♘g1** (the only square for the knight, but now the h1-rook gets trapped) **3...♗xg2** and Black wins material.

14) White cannot play d6 at once because the pawn is currently pinned, but the deflection **1 f4!** forces Black's queen away, and after **1...♕xf4 2 d6** White traps the rook.

15) White's rook is poorly placed and vulnerable to attack: **1...♔g7 2 ♖h5 ♖a8!** (preventing the rook from moving to h8 after ...♔g6) **3 ♔g3 ♔g6 4 ♔g4** and now Black can win the rook by **4...♖a4+** or **4...f5+**.

16) Black threatens ...♕f3+, but it is White who wins after **1 f3! exf3+** (or else the knight is captured straight away) **2 ♕xf3 ♕xf3+ 3 ♔xf3** (not 3 ♖xf3? allowing 3...♘c1) and the e2-knight is doomed.

17) White wins a piece by **1 ♖xh5 ♗xe3 2 ♘f1!**, unexpectedly snaring the bishop in the middle of the board.

18) **1 ♗c3+ ♔d1 2 ♖h1+ ♔c2** leads to Black's king blocking in his rook and now **3 ♔f3!** traps the enemy rook and wins.

19) **1 ♕c8+!** (not 1 ♖g4? ♕xg4+! 2 ♔xg4 ♘fe3+ 3 fxe3 ♘xe3+ and it is Black who wins) **1...♔h7 2 ♖g4** (possible now that the white queen is out of range of knight forks) **2...♘fe7** (the last try) **3 ♕f8** and the threat of mate on g7 ensures that Black will lose his queen.

20) Pieces can get trapped even in the endgame: **1 ♔d4 ♗a2** (1...♗a6 2 ♖b6+ and 1...♗e2 2 ♖e1 are also winning for White) **2 ♖b2 ♗d5 3 ♖b6+** and the bishop is lost.

21) Another venturesome queen comes to regret its solo trip into the enemy position: **1 ♖g1 ♕h3 2 ♗xf7+! ♔e7** (or 2...♔xf7 3 ♘g5+) **3 ♖g3** traps the queen.

22) White's queen lacks a path away from c6, but Black must choose the correct first move to be sure of trapping it. For example, 1...♕b3? attacks the a2-rook, but allows White to escape by 2 ♕c7 ♖e8 3 ♘c1, while 1...♕a7? 2 ♕b5! exploits the pin to get out. The only correct method is **1...♕b8! 2 b4** (there was no defence against the threat of 2...♗d7) **2...♗d7 3 bxc5 ♗xc6** and Black wins.

23) The knight can be trapped, but Black must take care: **1...♗e3+ 2 ♔g2 ♔e6!** (not 2...♗c5? 3 a4 ♔e6 4 a5 ♔d7 5 ♘b6+ and the knight escapes) **3 ♔f3 ♗g1** (3...♗c5 and 3...♗d4 are just as good) **4 ♔e4** (or 4 ♔g2 ♗c5 5 ♔f3 ♔d7 and the knight falls) **4...♔d7 5 ♔f5 ♔xc8 6 ♔g6 ♗d4** and Black wins.

24) A series of forced moves leads to Black's bishop being trapped: **1 ♗xd5! ♗xd5 2 e3 ♘e6 3 e4 fxe4 4 dxe4**. It's hard to see this sequence because the initial exchange of the powerful bishop on g2 looks very unlikely, and many strong players have overlooked it in analogous situations.

25) After **1...♕xc3+! 2 ♔xc3 ♘xe4+** Black not only saves the queen, but even wins a piece.

26) After **1...f4?** White can play **2 e3!**, which threatens both 3 ♕h5# and 3 exf4, and so wins a pawn. If then **2...h5**, intending 3 exf4 h4, the reply **3 ♗e2! ♘f6 4 exf4 h4 5 fxg5** wins material. Note that 2 e4? is inferior because the bishop remains trapped after 2...d6 3 ♕h5+ ♔d7.

27) **1 ♗xa7!** is a good move. After **1...b6** (otherwise White is just a pawn up) White plays **2 ♗b8!** (threatening to take another pawn) **2...♖xb8 3 ♖xe7** with a winning rook ending due to the extra pawn and the active rook on the seventh rank.

28) White can save the game with the ingenious **1 ♘f7!** (otherwise Black plays his bishop to g4 and then rounds up the knight; e.g., 1 ♔e3? ♗c2 2 ♔f4 ♗d1 3 ♔e4 ♗g4 4 ♔f4 ♔g7 and Black wins) **1...♔xf7 2 ♔g5 ♗g6** (or else Black's last pawn falls) **3 ♔h6!** and now **3...♔f6** is the only move to keep both bishop and pawn, but it stalemates White!

29) **1 ♕d5** is not effective here, because the idea of trapping the white queen on a8 (mentioned in Exercise 10) comes to Black's rescue: **1...♕c7! 2 ♕xa8 ♘c6** with the dangerous threat of ...♗b7. The best line for White is **3 ♗xb5 ♗b7 4 ♕xf8+ ♔xf8 5 ♗d3 ♘b4** with a roughly equal position.

30) After **1 a3**, the hidden idea **1...a5!** rescues the knight, since **2 axb4? axb4** attacks the c3-knight and the a1-rook, winning after **3 ♖xa8 ♗xc3** thanks to the pin on the white queen. Therefore White should not play 2 axb4?, but then Black continues ...♘a6 and remains a pawn up.

10 Pawn Promotion

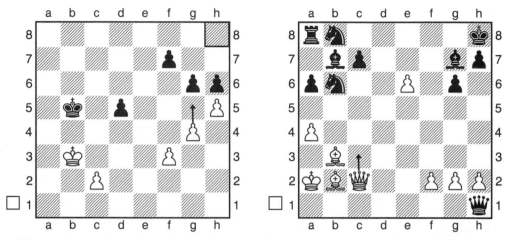

When a pawn promotes to a queen, the pawn disappears, costing you one point on the normal material scale (see page 5). But you also get a queen (worth nine points), winning eight points overall. This is such a large material gain that pawn promotion usually wins the game.

Tactics involving pawn promotion occur most frequently in the endgame, and the left-hand diagram above is an example. There are only the kings and a few pawns left, so if a pawn gets an unobstructed run to the eighth rank, it may well be impossible to stop. By playing **1 g5!**, White makes sure that one of his pawns will reach h8. The threat is 2 gxh6, which can only be prevented by **1...hxg5**. Then **2 h6** slips the h-pawn past the enemy pawns, and now the path is clear for the pawn to promote. Tactics such as this, with a sacrifice to clear the way for a pawn to run through, are called *breakthroughs* (see Exercise 3 for another example).

Even though pawn promotions occur most often in the endgame, they can also happen in the middlegame. In the right-hand diagram above, White has sacrificed a rook and two pieces for an attack on the enemy king, and his only chance is to force mate. He can achieve this by an amazing tactic, starting with **1 ♕c3!!**. Black must play **1...♗xc3**, as there's no other way to meet the threat of ♕xg7#, but then White continues **2 ♗xc3+ ♔g8 3 e7+ ♗d5 4 e8♕#**.

When a pawn promotes, it is usual to choose a queen for the promoted piece, as this gives the greatest gain of material. However, there are a few cases in which it is better to select a different piece. Sometimes a knight promotion is necessary, normally because you need to promote with check. In a very few positions, promotion to rook or even bishop is needed to avoid stalemating your opponent.

Here are some tips for solving the exercises:
- You may need to use one of the tactics from earlier chapters, such as deflection, to free your pawn to advance.
- Pawn promotions can occur as part of a mating attack. Exercise 4 is one example.
- Remember that you are allowed to promote to a rook, bishop or knight instead of a queen.

Exercises

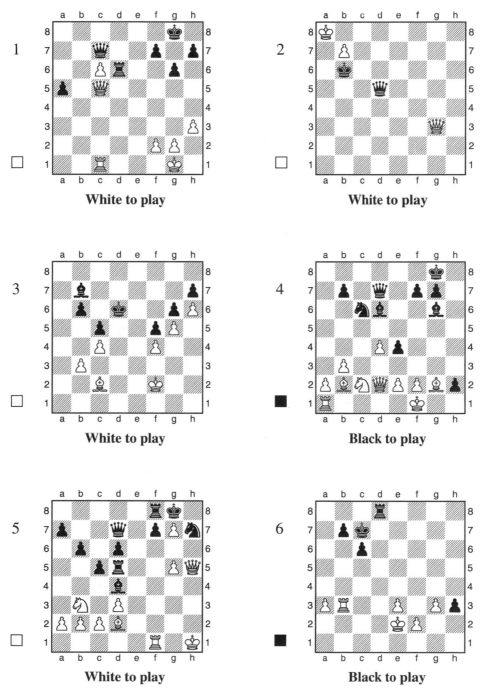

1 **White to play**

2 **White to play**

3 **White to play**

4 **Black to play**

5 **White to play**

6 **Black to play**

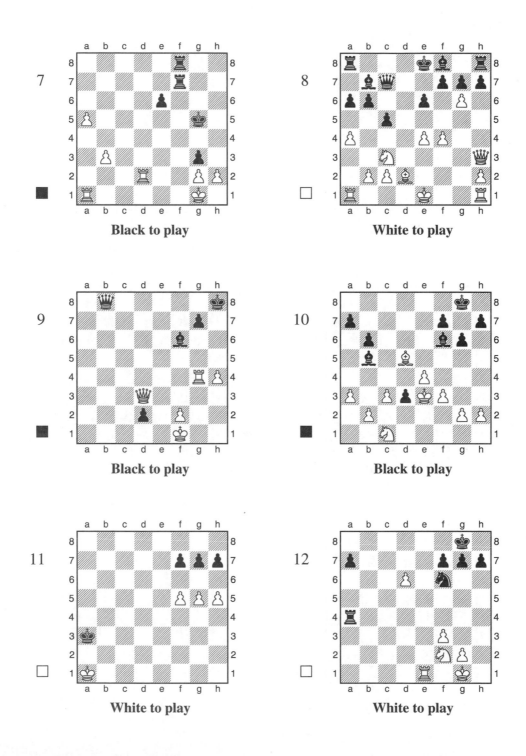

7 Black to play

8 White to play

9 Black to play

10 Black to play

11 White to play

12 White to play

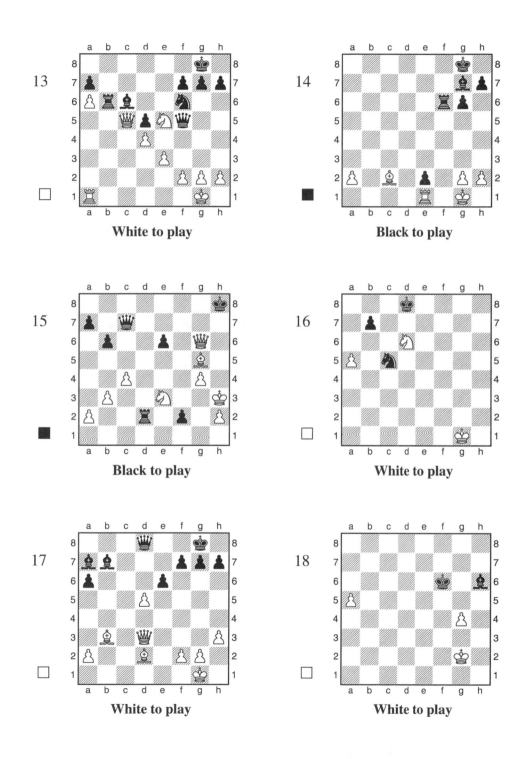

13   **White to play**

14   **Black to play**

15   **Black to play**

16   **White to play**

17   **White to play**

18   **White to play**

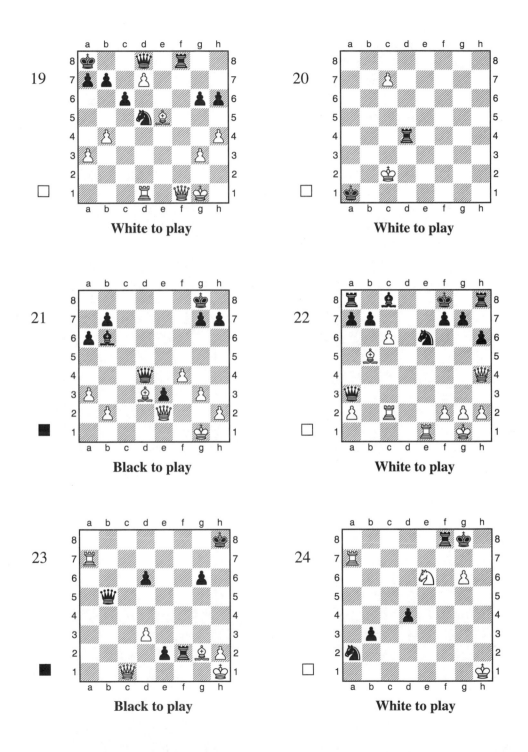

19

White to play

20

White to play

21

Black to play

22

White to play

23

Black to play

24

White to play

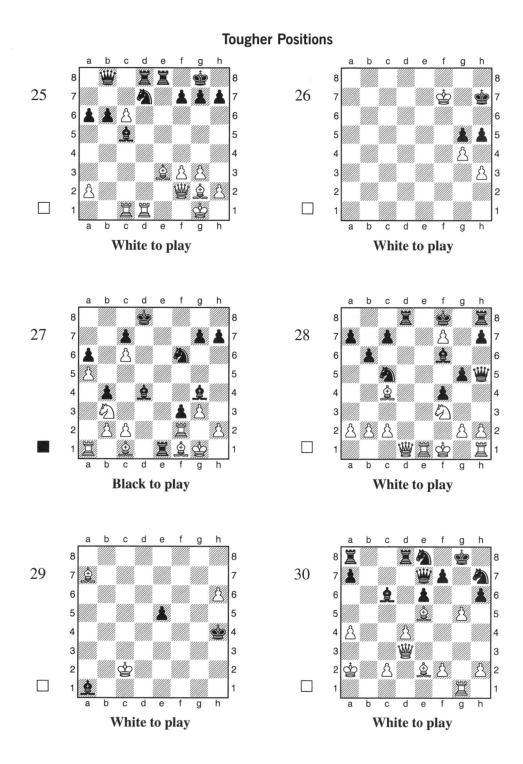

25 **White to play**

26 **White to play**

27 **Black to play**

28 **White to play**

29 **White to play**

30 **White to play**

Does the Tactic Work?

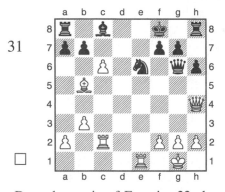

31

Does the tactic of Exercise 22 also win here?

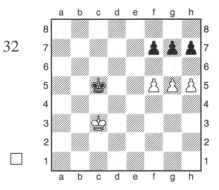

32

Does the breakthrough of Exercise 11 win?

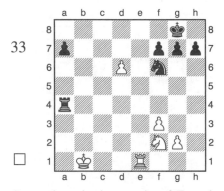

33

Does the winning tactic of Exercise 12 work in this position?

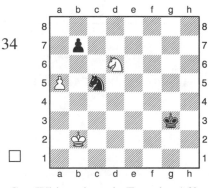

34

Can White win as in Exercise 16?

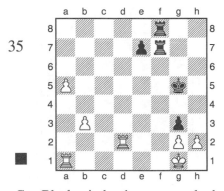

35

Can Black win by the same method as in Exercise 7?

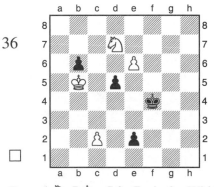

36

Does **1 ♘e5 ♔xe5 2 e7** win for White?

Solutions to Pawn Promotion Exercises

1) The blockade of the c6-pawn is broken by a sacrifice: **1 ♕xd6! ♕xd6 2 c7** and the pawn will promote, leaving White a rook ahead.

2) White's pawn is pinned, but a deflection not only relieves the pin, but also sets Black up for a skewer: **1 ♕b3+! ♕xb3 2 b8♕+** and **3 ♕xb3**. In only two moves, White combines deflection, decoy, skewer and pawn promotion.

3) White can blow up Black's fortress-like defences with a sacrifice: **1 ♗xf5! gxf5** (if Black doesn't take the bishop, White continues his demolition job with 2 ♗xg6!) **2 g6** and a pawn promotes; for example, **2...hxg6 3 h7** and **4 h8♕**. Sacrificial breakthroughs such as this often occur in the endgame to clear the way for a pawn to promote.

4) Despite being a rook down, Black can win by putting the dangerous h2-pawn to good use: **1...♕h3!** (pinning the bishop and ensuring the pawn's promotion) **2 ♗xh3 h1♕#**.

5) A clever knight promotion wins the game: **1 ♕xh7+!** (1 gxf8♕+? ♘xf8 only leads to an equal position) **1...♔xh7 2 gxf8♘+!** (not 2 gxf8♕?? ♕h3#) followed by **3 ♘xd7** leaves White two pieces ahead. Promoting to a piece other than the queen is called *underpromotion*, and although it is only rarely necessary, there are a few situations where it is essential.

6) After 1...h2? 2 ♖b1 ♖h8 3 ♖h1 the passed pawn is stopped, but **1...♖d1!** makes sure the pawn will reach h1. The threat is simply 2...h2 and **2 ♔xd1 h2** followed by **3...h1♕** will leave White queen for rook and pawn down.

7) Black can make use of his far-advanced g3-pawn with a rook sacrifice: **1...♖f1+! 2 ♖xf1 ♖xf1+ 3 ♔xf1 gxh2** and the pawn promotes, giving Black a decisive material advantage.

8) White wins with a tactic that can occur in several different situations: **1 ♕xh7! ♖xh7 2 gxh7** and Black cannot prevent the pawn from promoting, so White wins a rook.

9) White is ahead on material, but Black can turn the tables by **1...♕b5! 2 ♕xb5** (2 ♖c4 d1♕+ 3 ♕xd1 ♕xc4+ also wins for Black) **2...d1♕+ 3 ♔g2 ♕xg4+** and Black is a piece up.

10) The path to victory involves a combination of various tactics: **1...♗g5+** skewers the king and knight, so White must play **2 f4** but then the deflection **2...♗xf4+!** draws the white king away from d2. After **3 ♔xf4 d2** the pawn will promote on c1 or d1.

11) White wins with a textbook pawn breakthrough: **1 g6!** (any other move is met by ...g6 and the chance of a breakthrough has gone) **1...fxg6** (or the mirror-image line 1...hxg6 2 f6! gxf6 3 h6) **2 h6! gxh6 3 f6** and White promotes well before Black.

12) This is another standard idea well worth knowing: **1 ♖e8+! ♘xe8 2 d7** and, thanks to the preliminary sacrifice, there are now two possible promotion squares for the pawn. Black cannot cover both, so White will be queen for rook (and two pawns) up.

13) Black's pieces are badly placed and after **1 ♕xb6! axb6 2 ♘xc6** he cannot stop the a-pawn. The only realistic try is **2...♕c8**, heading for a8, but this loses to the fork **3 ♘e7+**.

14) Black must strike at once or he will lose the far-advanced pawn: **1...♖f1+! 2 ♖xf1 ♗d4+ 3 ♖f2** (or 3 ♔h1 exf1♕#) **3...e1♕#**.

15) White is threatening ♗f6+, but Black can strike first: **1...♕xh2+!** (1...f1♕+? 2 ♘xf1 defends h2) **2 ♔xh2 f1♕+** (2...f1♘++? 3 ♔g1 wins for White) **3 ♔g3 ♕f2+ 4 ♔h3** and now the quickest mate is **4...♕h2#**.

97

16) White wins using a typical promotion tactic: **1 ♘xb7+! ♘xb7** (or 1...♔c7 2 ♘xc5 ♔c6 3 a6 ♔b6 4 ♔f2 and White wins by supporting the pawn with his king) **2 a6 ♔c7 3 a7** and the black knight blocks the very square needed by Black's king, so the pawn promotes.

17) This harmless-seeming position conceals a decisive tactical blow: **1 dxe6! ♛xd3** (there's not much choice as White was threatening both 2 exf7+ and 2 ♛xd8#) **2 exf7+ ♔f8** (or 2...♔h8 3 f8♛#) **3 ♗b4+** with mate in two more moves.

18) The immediate 1 a6? is met by 1...♗e3, while 1 ♔f3? ♗f8 followed by ...♗c5 stops the a-pawn, so White must first prevent the bishop from moving to the g1-a7 diagonal: **1 g5+! ♗xg5** (or 1...♔xg5 2 a6 and the pawn promotes) **2 ♔f3!** and, surprisingly, there's no way the bishop can cover a7 in time to stop the pawn promoting.

19) White wins with a tricky tactic: **1 ♛xf8! ♛xf8 2 ♗c7!** (this is the hard move to see; it threatens to promote and if Black takes the bishop the d-file is opened) **2...♘xc7** (or else 3 d8♛+ will leave White a rook up) **3 d8♛+ ♛xd8 4 ♖xd8#**.

20) In very rare cases, a rook promotion is necessary: **1 c8♖!!** (1 c8♛? allows 1...♖c4+! 2 ♛xc4 with a draw by stalemate, while 1 ♔b3 makes no progress as Black can repeat the position by 1...♖d3+ 2 ♔c2 ♖d4) **1...♖a4** (this is the only way to defend against the threat of mate by 2 ♖a8+ without losing the rook immediately; the key point is that 1...♖c4+ 2 ♖xc4 is not stalemate) **2 ♔b3** creates two new threats of 3 ♖c1# and 3 ♔xa4, and so wins Black's rook.

21) A sacrifice sets the e3-pawn in motion, but there is a twist at the end: **1...♛xd3! 2 ♛xd3 e2+ 3 ♔g2** (after 3 ♔h1 e1♛+ 4 ♔g2 ♛e6 Black has an extra piece) **3...e1♘+!** followed by **4...♘xd3**, with two extra pieces for Black. The knight promotion is essential, since 3...e1♛? 4 ♛b3+ ♔h8 5 ♛xb6 leaves White a pawn ahead.

22) Not all tactics fit into standard patterns. This is one of the more unusual ones, although it is made up of familiar building-blocks: **1 ♛d8+!!** (deflection, pulling the defensive knight away) **1...♘xd8 2 cxb7** (a discovered attack, opening the line from b5 to e8 to threaten ♖e8#) **2...♗e6 3 bxa8♛** and White is now material up with a strong attack.

23) Some imagination is required to work out how to exploit the e2-pawn: **1...♖f1+! 2 ♗xf1** (2 ♛xf1 exf1♛+ 3 ♗xf1 is hopeless since 3...♛c6+ 4 ♔g1 ♛b6+ picks up the rook) **2...♛c6+!** (this deflection draws the white queen away from guarding f1; not 2...♛d5+? 3 ♗g2) **3 ♛xc6 exf1♛#**.

24) **1 ♖g7+** (1 ♘xf8? ♔xf8 2 ♖b7 ♘c1 is only a draw as White will lose his last pawn while he is dealing with Black's pawns) **1...♔h8** and now White could win by g7+ except that his rook is blocking that square. The solution is to get rid of the rook by **2 ♖h7+ ♔g8 3 ♖h8+! ♔xh8** (the same position as before, except that the rook has vanished) and now **4 g7+** followed by **5 gxf8♛** wins.

25) White needs to find the correct sequence to exploit his c6-pawn: **1 ♖xd7!** (after 1 cxd7? ♗xe3 2 dxe8♛+ ♖xe8 White wins a rook but loses his queen) **1...♗xe3** (1...♖xd7 loses to 2 cxd7 ♗xe3 3 ♛xe3 ♖xe4 4 ♖c8+) **2 ♛xe3! ♖xe3 3 c7** and the attacks on b8 and d8 guarantee that White will come out at least a piece up.

26) White plays to create a passed g-pawn: **1 h4!** (1 ♔f6? hxg4 2 hxg4 ♔g8 3 ♔g5 ♔g7 is a standard draw) **1...♔h6** (1...gxh4 2 g5 is the same as the main line after 4 ♔f7, while 1...hxg4 2 hxg5 g3 3 g6+ ♔h6 4 g7 g2 5 g8♛ wins for White) **2 ♔f6!** (now hxg5+ is a threat, so Black must make a pawn capture) **2...gxh4** (2...hxg4 3 hxg5+ ♔h7 4 ♔f7 g3 5 g6+ and White wins as before) **3 g5+ ♔h7 4 ♔f7! h3 5 g6+ ♔h6 6 g7 h2 7 g8♕ h1♕ 8 ♕g7#** (or 8 ♕g6#).

27) Two white pieces are blocking the f-pawn's advance, but the correct sequence of moves can eliminate both of them: **1...♗xf2+ 2 ♔xf2 ♘e4+! 3 ♔g1** (3 ♔xe1 f2# is a neat mate) **3...♖xf1+** (the second defender bites the dust) **4 ♔xf1 ♗h3+ 5 ♔e1** (or 5 ♔g1 f2+ 6 ♔h1 f1♕#) **5...f2+ 6 ♔e2 f1♕+** and Black is not only queen for rook up but also has a deadly attack.

28) White forces mate with a deep tactic: **1 ♕xd8+!** (the first step is to eliminate the rook which was controlling e8) **1...♗xd8 2 ♖e8+ ♔g7 3 ♖g8+! ♖xg8** (or 3...♔f6 4 f8♕+ ♕f7 5 ♕xf7#) **4 fxg8♕+** and White mates in two more moves: **4...♔h6 5 ♕f8+ ♔g6 6 ♘e5#** or **4...♔f6 5 ♕f8+ ♔g6 6 ♘e5#**.

29) White aims to prevent Black from controlling h8 with his bishop: **1 ♗d4!!** (a really surprising move, but not 1 h7? e4, solving all Black's problems) **1...♗xd4** (1...exd4 2 ♔d3! firmly shuts the a1-h8 diagonal) **2 ♔d3** (the bishop is undefended on d4, so Black cannot play ...e4+ at once) **2...♗a1 3 ♔e4!**, preventing ...e4, followed by **4 h7** and White wins.

30) Pawn-promotion tactics can be quite intricate. 1 gxh6+? ♔f8 2 ♕xh7 looks dangerous, but after 2...♕b4 Black's king can slip away to e7. The correct sequence is: **1 ♕xh7+!!** (first the queen sacrifice...) **1...♔xh7 2 ♗d3+ ♔g8** (2...f5 3 gxf6+ ♔h8 4 fxe7+ leads to catastrophe for Black) **3 gxh6+ ♔f8** (...and now the deadly follow-up) **4 ♖g8+! ♔xg8 5 h7+ ♔f8 6 h8♕#**.

31) The tactic **1 ♕d8+? ♘xd8 2 cxb7** doesn't work here as **2...♕xg2+! 3 ♔xg2 ♗xb7+** followed by ...♘e6 leaves Black a piece up. Spotting tactics by your opponent is often just as important as finding ideas for yourself.

32) Here **1 g6** only leads to a draw, but there is nothing better for White. The continuation is **1...fxg6!** (not 1...hxg6? 2 f6! gxf6 3 h6 and the h-pawn promotes) **2 hxg6** (White loses after 2 h6? gxh6 3 f6 ♔d6 because Black's king is close enough to stop the f-pawn) **2...hxg6** (not 2...h5? 3 f6) **3 fxg6** and with careful play it is a draw. For example, **3...♔d5 4 ♔d3 ♔e5 5 ♔e3 ♔f5 6 ♔f3 ♔xg6 7 ♔g4** with a standard textbook draw.

33) Here **1 ♖e8+?** is actually a losing blunder due to **1...♘xe8 2 d7 ♖b4+! 3 ♔a2 ♖b8**, when Black covers both d8 and e8, and has a winning material advantage.

34) Here the tactic **1 ♘xb7 ♘xb7 2 a6** doesn't promote the pawn since Black can continue **2...♘d6** (2...♘a5 and 2...♘c5 draw the same way, as in both cases the knight can reach b6 with the aid of a check) **3 a7 ♘c4+! 4 ♔c3 ♘b6**, stopping the pawn. Then White's only winning attempt is to advance his king, but although **5 ♔b4 ♔f4 6 ♔b5 ♘a8 7 ♔c6 ♔e5 8 ♔b7 ♔d6 9 ♔xa8 ♔c7** leads to the win of the knight, White has got himself stalemated.

35) The tactic of Exercise 7 doesn't work here. The small change of having the pawn on e7 instead of e6 makes a big difference. **1...♖f1+ 2 ♔xf1 ♖xf1+ 3 ♔xf1 gxh2 4 ♖d5+** (here d5 is not covered by Black's pawn) **4...♔g6 5 ♖h5!! ♔xh5 6 g4+ ♔xg4 7 ♔g2** and White stops the h-pawn, after which his a-pawn promotes. It's important to treat every position individually. Just because one position is similar to another doesn't guarantee that the same ideas will work.

36) It does win, but only because of a cunning idea: **1 ♘e5!** (threatening 2 ♘d3+) **1...♔xe5** (1...e1♕ 2 ♘d3+ is an easy win) **2 e7 e1♕** (everything is set for a skewer, but there is a trap) **3 e8♖+!!** (the trap is 3 e8♕+? ♔d4! 4 ♕xe1 and Black is stalemated) **3...♔d4 4 ♖xe1** and White wins.

99

11 Opening and Closing Lines

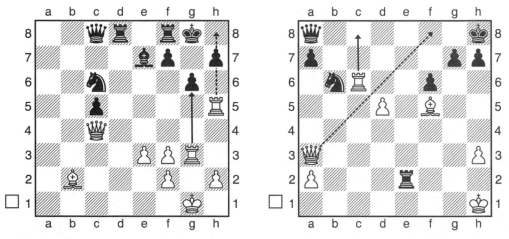

Many chess tactics are based on opening or closing lines. Three pieces, the queen, rook and bishop, move along straight lines and anything that blocks or clears lines will have an impact on the mobility of these pieces. In the left-hand diagram above, White's b2-bishop and h5-rook are both aimed towards h8, and if the pawn on h7 were not there then White could mate immediately by ♖h8#. White can blast the line h5-h8 open with the rook sacrifice **1 ♖xg6+!**. The pawn on f7 is pinned by the white queen, so Black's reply **1...hxg6** is forced, but then White can play **2 ♖h8#**. Here the *line-opening tactic* is based on removing an enemy piece, but sometimes, as in Exercise 6 below, it's your own piece that has to be cleared out of the way.

The opposite of a line-opening tactic is a *line-closing tactic*. The right-hand diagram above is a good example. White could mate by ♕f8#, except that this square is covered by the black queen from a8. If White could close the line between a8 and f8, then he could deliver immediate mate. The sacrifice **1 ♖c8+!** is the key move. After **1...♘xc8** the black queen no longer guards f8, and White plays **2 ♕f8#**. Playing **1...♕xc8** doesn't help Black, as **2 ♗xc8 ♘xc8** (or else Black is queen for rook down) **3 ♕f8#** is still mate.

The exercises in this chapter include many variations on the line-opening and line-closing themes, so you may find the winning move harder to spot than in some other chapters. However, these tips should help you:

- Look for forcing moves that open or close lines. Does this make something possible that was impossible before?
- Try 'what if' scenarios. For example, what if a particular pawn weren't there? How can you get it out of the way?
- Sometimes it is your own piece that is in the way. If so, work out how you can get rid of the piece with gain of time.

Exercises

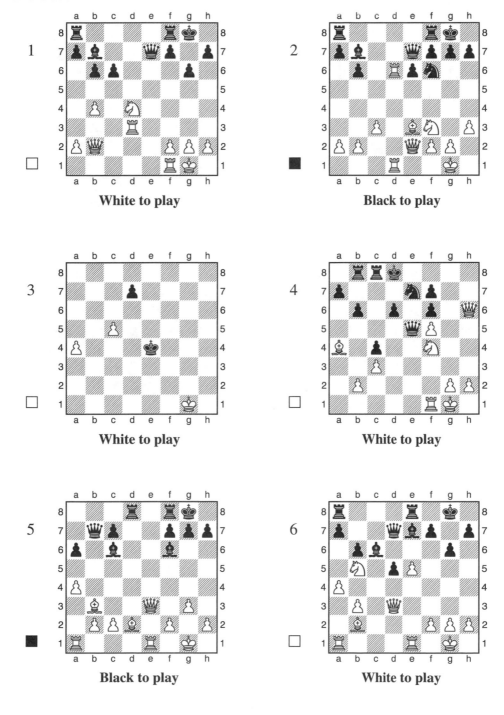

1 White to play

2 Black to play

3 White to play

4 White to play

5 Black to play

6 White to play

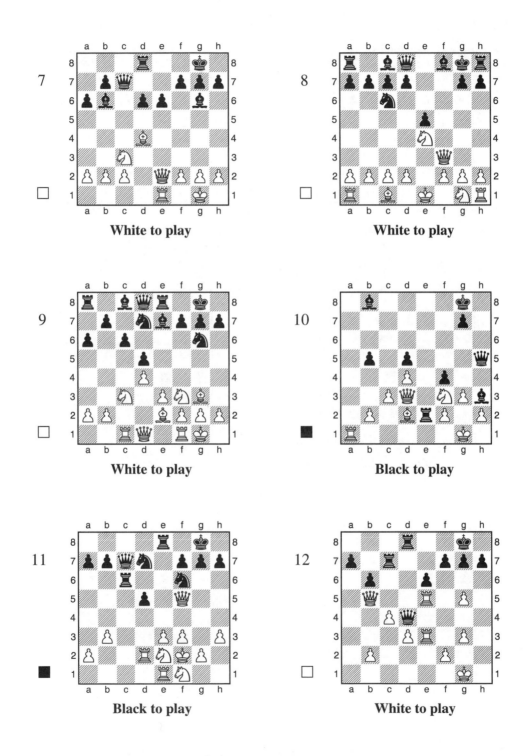

7 White to play

8 White to play

9 White to play

10 Black to play

11 Black to play

12 White to play

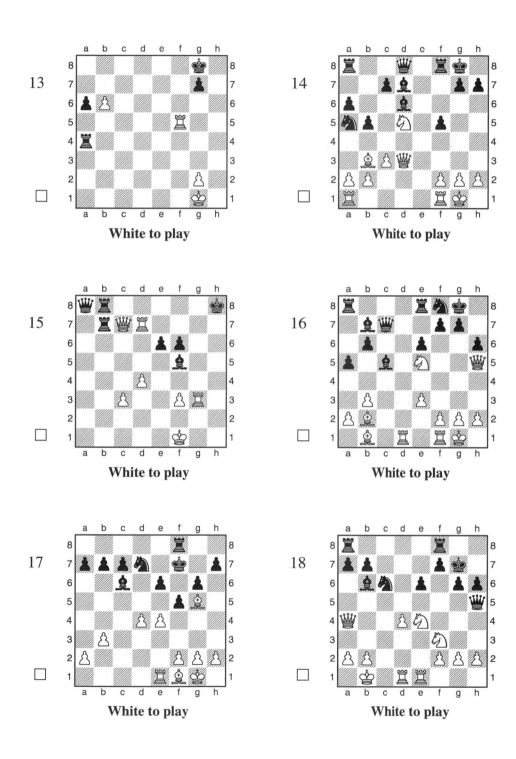

13

White to play

14

White to play

15

White to play

16

White to play

17

White to play

18

White to play

103

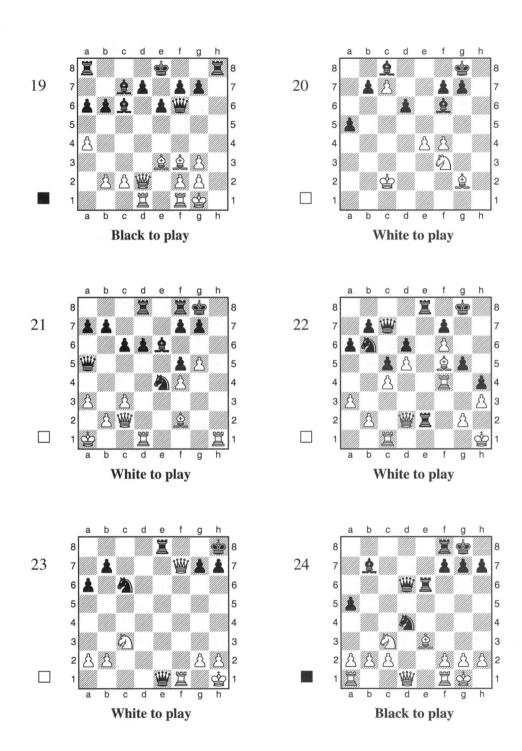

19

Black to play

20

White to play

21

White to play

22

White to play

23

White to play

24

Black to play

Tougher Positions

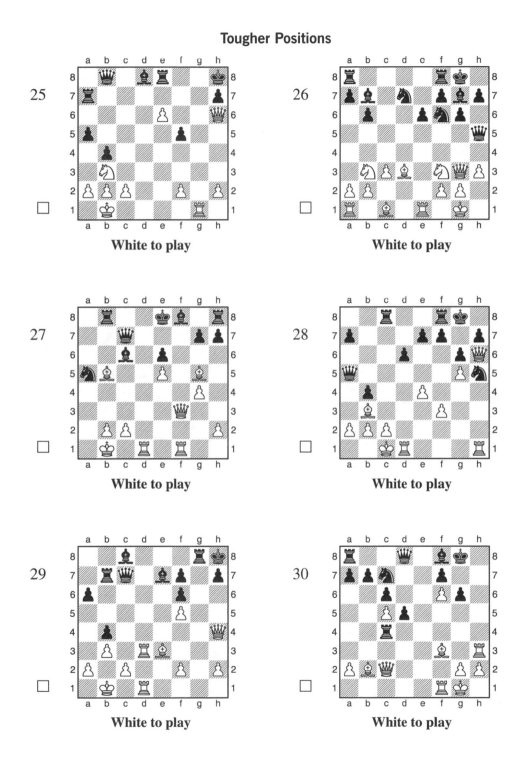

25 — White to play

26 — White to play

27 — White to play

28 — White to play

29 — White to play

30 — White to play

31

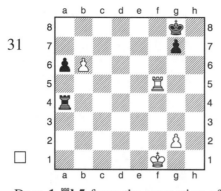

Does **1 ♖b5** force the promotion of the pawn?

32

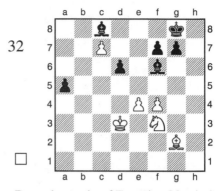

Does the tactic of Exercise 20 win here?

33

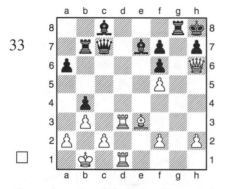

Does the win of Exercise 29 work here?

34

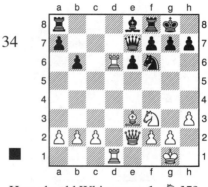

How should White meet **1...♘d5**?

35

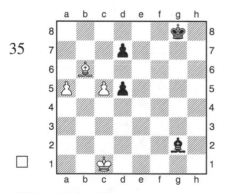

White tried to block the diagonal by **1 c6 dxc6 2 a6**, hoping to promote his pawn. How should Black reply?

36

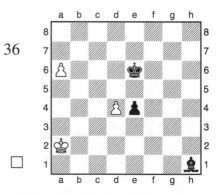

White played **1 d5+**. What is the correct result of the game?

Solutions to Opening and Closing Lines Exercises

1) A quick strike opens the g-file for the white rook: **1 ♞f5!** (threatening the queen and 2 ♕g7#) **1...gxf5 2 ♖g3+** and mate next move.

2) The d6-rook may look active, but actually it is in an exposed position: **1...♞d5!** cuts off the rook's support and traps it, winning at least rook for knight.

3) There are no line-moving pieces here, so how can there be a line-closing tactic? The point is that 1 a5? ♔d5 2 a6 ♔c6 3 a7 ♔b7 doesn't win because the black king can reach a8 by moving along the line e4-a8. The solution is **1 c6! dxc6 2 a5 ♔d5 3 a6**, winning because the diagonal line to a8 is now blocked by the black pawn.

4) A sacrifice blocks the line from e5 to e7, so that the e7-knight will be undefended later on: **1 ♞e6+! fxe6 2 ♕f8+ ♔c7 3 ♕xe7#**.

5) By 'overshooting' the square g2, Black opens the diagonal for his queen: **1...♗h1!** (threatening 2...♕g2#) **2 f3** (the only defence, but it allows a deadly pin) **2....♗d4**, winning the white queen.

6) The long diagonal leading to Black's king provides a ready-made line of attack and White only needs to open it with gain of time: **1 e6! fxe6 2 ♕d4** (threatening mate at g7; not 2 ♕c3? d4 3 ♞xd4 ♗f6, letting Black off the hook) **2....♗f8** (this only delays mate by a couple of moves) **3 ♕h8+ ♔f7 4 ♕xh7+ ♗g7 5 ♕xg7#**.

7) Black's position looks sound enough, but White can lob a bomb into it with a knight sacrifice: **1 ♞d5!** (forking queen and bishop, so Black must take or lose a piece) **1...exd5** (now the e-file is opened) **2 ♕e8+ ♖xe8 3 ♖xe8#**.

8) **1 ♞g5!** not only threatens 2 ♕f7#, but by opening the line from f3 to d5 creates a second threat of 2 ♕d5#. Black cannot meet both threats, and loses after **1...♕xg5 2 ♕d5#** or **1...♕e7 2 ♕d5+ ♕e6 3 ♞xe6**.

9) This is a standard opening trap which can occur in several similar positions. White makes off with an important central pawn by **1 ♞xd5!** since **1...cxd5? 2 ♗c7** costs Black his queen. The knight sacrifice was needed to open the c-file so that the bishop is defended on c7.

10) Black wants to mate on g2, but the white queen is defending the knight and so prevents ...♕xf3. **1...♖e3!** is the solution and after **2 fxe3** (2 ♗xe3 ♕xf3 is similar) **2...♕xf3** White can only prevent mate by giving up his queen.

11) A sacrifice opening the f-file lays the groundwork for a nasty pin: **1...♞e4+!** (forking king and rook, so White must take) **2 fxe4 ♖f6** and White loses his queen for rook and knight.

12) White's plan is to open the e-file so he can crash through on e8: **1 ♖d5! exd5** (or 1...♖xd5 2 ♕e8#) **2 ♖e8+** (2 ♕e8+ is just as good) **2...♖xe8 3 ♕xe8#**.

13) Line-closing tactics can just as easily arise in the endgame. 1 b7? ♖b4 leads nowhere, so White first has to block the b-file by **1 ♖b5! axb5** (if Black does not take, then White plays b7 in any case) and only then play **2 b7**. The pawn will promote, giving White a decisive material advantage.

14) White is a piece down but a double check plus line-opening tactic forces mate: **1 ♞e7++ ♔h8 2 ♞g6+!** (opening the h-file) **2...hxg6 3 ♕h3+ ♕h4 4 ♕xh4#**.

15) **1 ♖g8+!** (opening the diagonal for the queen to move to h2) **1...♔xg8** (or 1...♖xg8 2 ♕h2+) **2 ♕g3+ ♔f8** (2...♔h8 3 ♕g7#) **3 ♕g7+ ♔e8** and now **4 ♕e7#** or **4 ♕f7#**.

16) **1 ♖d7!** (cutting off the black queen's guard of f7) **1...♘xd7 2 ♕xf7+ ♚h8 3 ♘g6+ ♚h7 4 ♕xg7#.**

17) White plays to open the e-file and get his rook to e7: **1 d5!** (Black's bishop has no safe square, so he must take) **1...exd5 2 exd5 ♗xd5 3 ♖e7+ ♚g8 4 ♖xd7** and the fork has won White a piece.

18) White wins by a combination of line-opening and line-closing: **1 d5! exd5** (1...♘e5 2 ♘g3 ♕g4 3 ♖e4 also traps the queen) **2 ♘g3** and the black queen is trapped. White's preliminary d5 advance has both closed the fifth rank, preventing the queen from escaping horizontally, and opened the fourth rank, which prevents the queen from fleeing to g4.

19) 1...♗xf3? is tempting, but 2 ♕xd7+ (not 2 gxf3?? ♕xf3 3 ♕xd7+ ♚f8 and Black wins) 2...♚f8 3 ♕xc7 ♗xd1 4 ♖xd1 is only equal. The solution is the dramatic **1...♕xf3! 2 gxf3 ♗xf3**, blasting open the diagonal leading to h1. The threat of 3...♖h1# can only be met by **3 ♗h6** (after 3 ♕xd7+ ♚f8, mate is unavoidable) **3...♖xh6 4 ♕xh6 gxh6**, but then White is well down on material.

20) Black's bishop is drawn away to h3, and then the line between h3 and c8 is shut: **1 ♗h3! ♗xh3 2 f5** and the c-pawn promotes.

21) A queen switch to the h-file will force mate, but the bishop must be moved with gain of time or else Black will be able to defend: **1 ♗b6!** (opening the line from c2 to h2 while attacking the black queen; 1 ♗e3? is too slow and allows the king to slip away by 1...♖fe8 2 ♕h2 ♚f8) **1...♕xb6 2 ♕h2 f6** (this only staves off the end by one move) **3 g6** followed by mate.

22) White's queen is under attack, but this doesn't matter if he finds the correct move: **1 ♖e4!!** (opening the line from d2 to g5 and at the same time preventing ...♖xd2) **1...♖8xe4** (White also mates after 1...♖xd2 2 ♖xe8# or 1...♖2xe4 2 ♕xg5+ ♚f8 3 ♕g7#) **2 ♕xg5+ ♚f8 3 ♕g7+ ♚e8 4 ♕g8#.**

23) White can't take the enemy queen, since 1 ♖xe1?? even loses after 1...♖xe1+. 1 ♕f8+? ♖xf8 fails because White's rook is pinned, while 1 h3? is too slow and lets Black escape by 1...♕e7. The solution lies in a clever line-closing move: **1 ♘e4!** (attacking both rook and queen; 1 ♘e2! is just as good and wins in the same way) **1...♕xe4** (1...♖xe4 2 ♕f8#) **2 ♕f8+ ♖xf8 3 ♖xf8#.**

24) Black's initial sacrifice opens the g-file and paves the way for a ferocious attack: **1...♘f3+! 2 gxf3** (or 2 ♚h1 ♕xh2#) **2...♖g6+ 3 ♚h1 ♕xd1** followed by **4...♗xf3#.**

25) The a7-rook covers the mate by ♕g7#, while the d8-bishop prevents ♕f6+. The lines a7-g7 and d8-f6 cross at e7, so it's the perfect place for White to throw a spanner in the works by **1 e7!**. Now it's mate in at most two more moves; for example, **1...♖exe7 2 ♕f8#**, **1...♗xe7 2 ♕g7#**, **1...♖axe7 2 ♕f6+ ♖g7 3 ♕xg7#** or **1...♕e5 2 ♕f8+! ♖xf8 3 exf8♕#.**

26) White can box in the enemy queen by **1 ♘g5!**, which closes the fifth rank and so prevents the queen from escaping to d5. The threat is 2 ♗e2 ♕h6 and then 3 ♘xf7 or 3 ♘xe6. Perhaps surprisingly, there's nothing Black can do to prevent this.

27) Black's king is in dire danger and one spectacular move is all it takes to push White's attack home: **1 ♗e7!!** (blocking the line from c7 to f7 and so threatening 2 ♕f7#) **1...♕xe7** (1...♚xe7 and 1...♗xe7 do not prevent the mate on f7) **2 ♗xc6+ ♘xc6 3 ♕xc6+** and mate next move.

28) White can use a typical kingside demolition to open up the g-file: **1 ♖xh5! gxh5 2 g6** (the pin on the f-pawn proves disastrous for Black) **2...hxg6 3 ♕xg6+ ♔h8 4 ♕h6+ ♔g8 5 ♖g1+** and mate next move.

29) White starts by opening the third rank to allow his rook to reach h3, then finishes with a discovered-check combination we have seen before (Exercise 13 on page 59): **1 ♗f4** (gaining time by attacking the queen) **1...♕c6** (there is nothing better) **2 ♕xh7+! ♔xh7 3 ♖h3+ ♔g7 4 ♗h6+ ♔h7 5 ♗f8#**.

30) Drastic measures are required to open the long diagonal for a mate on h8: **1 ♕xg6+!! fxg6 2 ♗xd5+!** (White needs to open the f-file as well, so that his rook can support the f-pawn) **2...♕xd5** (or 2...♘xd5 3 f7#) **3 f7+ ♕xf7 4 ♖h8#**.

31) Here **1 ♖b5?** is a blunder which loses after **1...axb5 2 b7 ♖f4+!** (this check allows Black to stop the pawn) **3 ♔g1 ♖f8**. The small difference from Exercise 13 (king on f1 instead of g1) totally changes the position.

32) Unlike Exercise 20, here **1 ♗h3?** is a blunder because after **1...♗xh3 2 f5** Black can get back to stop the pawn by **2...♗f1+ 3 ♔e3 ♗a6**, leaving him a piece up.

33) In contrast to the similar Exercise 29, here Black has a way out: **1 ♗f4 ♗f8!** (this counterattack saves the day) **2 ♕h4** (after 2 ♕xf6+? ♗g7 Black consolidates his extra piece, while 2 ♕xh7+? ♔xh7 3 ♖h3+ ♗h6! 4 ♖xh6+ ♔g7 is also winning for Black) **2...♕c6** with an equal position. Best play is actually **3 ♖d6! ♕c3 4 ♖6d3 ♕c6** with a draw by repetition.

34) This is similar to Exercise 2, but here White has an escape route after **1...♘d5**. The spectacular reply **2 ♗c5!** not only avoids loss of material but even gives White a slight advantage. After **2...bxc5 3 ♖6xd5** White regains the piece thanks to the e-file pin, so the best line for Black is **2...♘c3** (at least doubling White's pawns) **3 bxc3 bxc5 4 ♕c4**, but even here White is a little better as his active pieces are more important than his weakened pawns.

35) After **1 c6 dxc6 2 a6** Black can save the game by **2...c5!** (Black must play his moves in the correct order as after 2...d4? 3 ♗c5 the pawn does indeed promote) **3 ♗xc5** (or 3 a7 d4) **3...d4** and the a-pawn is stopped, when Black draws.

36) After **1 d5+** one black move wins, another draws and all the others lose. 1...♔d6? leads to a draw after 2 ♔b3! e3 3 ♔c3 e2 4 ♔d2 ♗f3 5 a7 ♗xd5 6 ♔xe2, eliminating Black's only pawn. The better **1...♔e5!** wins, since after **2 ♔b3** (2 a7 e3 3 a8♕ ♗xd5+ wins the queen, after which the e-pawn promotes) **2...e3 3 ♔c3 ♗xd5 4 ♔d3** Black's king is near enough to defend the pawn by **4...♔f4**. All of Black's other first moves don't stop the a-pawn and so lose.

CLOSING LINES

12 Forcing a Draw

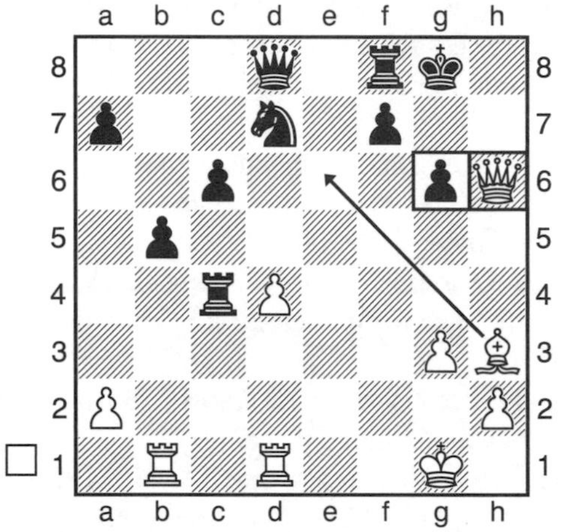

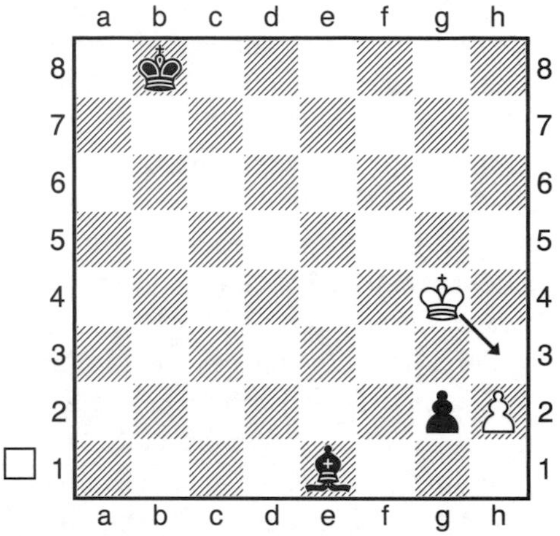

The standard scoring system for chess gives you one point for a win, half a point for a draw and zero for a loss. So drawing a lost position gains you half a point, the same as winning a drawn position. One method of rescuing a bad position is *perpetual check*. This involves continually checking the enemy king so that the position is repeated. The left-hand diagram above is an example. White is a pawn down and is in danger of losing, but he makes use of the active position of his queen by playing **1 ♗e6!**. This threatens both 2 ♗xc4 and 2 ♕xg6+ (because the f7-pawn is now pinned), so Black is forced to take the bishop by **1...fxe6**. Then **2 ♕xg6+ ♚h8 3 ♕h6+ ♚g8 4 ♕g6+** is perpetual check. The position is repeated again and again, and by the rules of chess this is a draw. It's also possible to chase a piece other than the king backwards and forwards. This is called a *perpetual attack* (Exercise 3 is one example).

If you have no legal moves, but your king is not attacked, that is *stalemate* and according to the rules the game is an immediate draw. In the right-hand diagram above, Black's pawn is about to become a queen. It looks like White is on the brink of defeat, but now he plays **1 ♔h3!**. The g2-pawn is attacked but promoting to rook or queen is stalemate. Two dark-squared bishops are no more useful than one, so Black's only chance is to promote to a knight by **1...g1♘+**. Now **2 ♔g2** exploits the clumsy position of Black's pieces and after **2...♘e2 3 ♔f1** one of them is doomed, leaving Black with *insufficient material* to win.

Here are some tips for solving the exercises:

- Some of the exercises involve a small amount of endgame knowledge. For example, you need to know when a position of king and pawn against king is a draw. You also need to know that king and two knights against king (without any other material) is a draw and that queen against rook (again with no other material) is generally a win. If you need to revise your endgames, you can consult *Chess Endgames for Kids* (Gambit, 2015).
- To give perpetual check, you may need to start with a sacrifice to expose the enemy king.
- Stalemates can easily be overlooked, so keep your eyes open!

Exercises

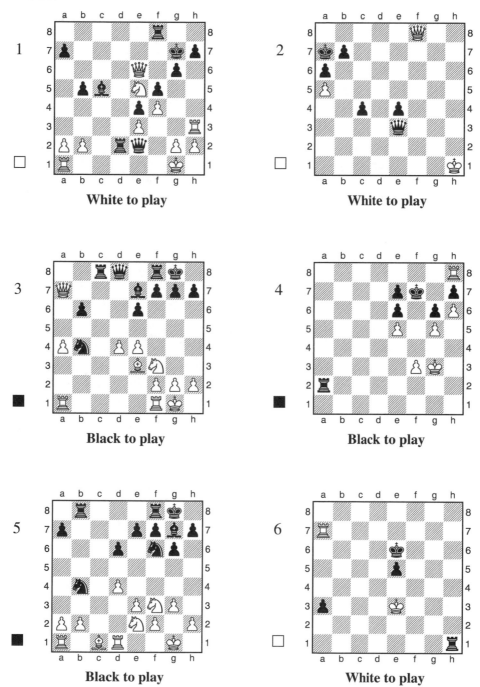

1   **White to play**

2   **White to play**

3   **Black to play**

4   **Black to play**

5   **Black to play**

6   **White to play**

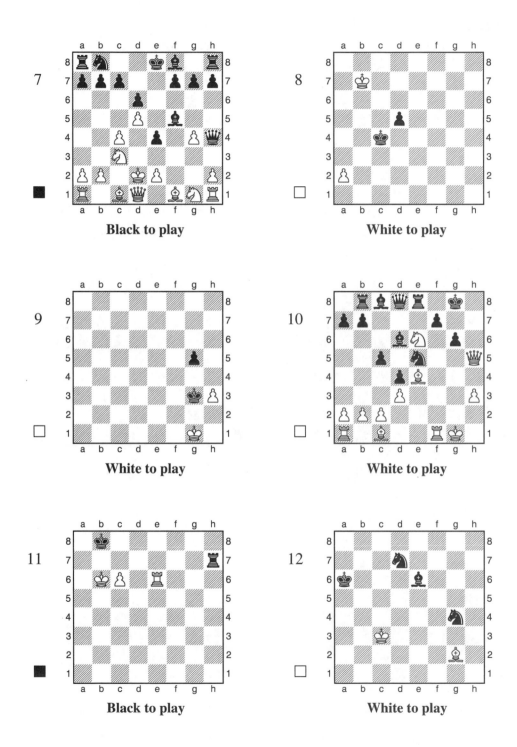

7

Black to play

8

White to play

9

White to play

10

White to play

11

Black to play

12

White to play

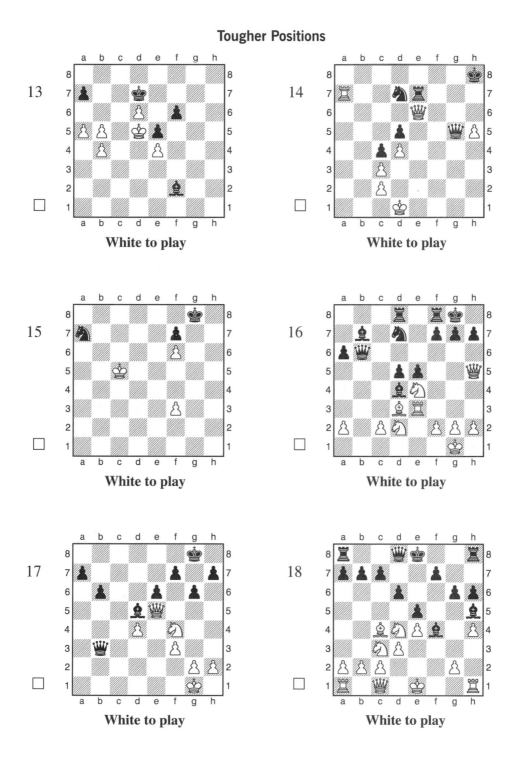

13 White to play

14 White to play

15 White to play

16 White to play

17 White to play

18 White to play

Does the Tactic Work?

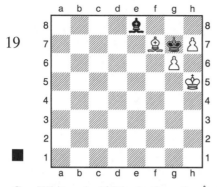

19

Can White win if Black plays **1...♗xf7 2 gxf7 ♔xh7**?

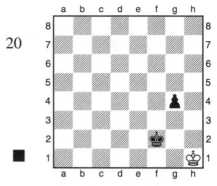

20

1...g3 is stalemate, but can Black win with another move?

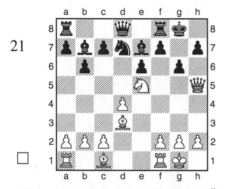

21

White tried to force a draw by **1 ♘xg6**, with the idea of **1...hxg6 2 ♗xg6 fxg6 3 ♕xg6+**. Was this a good idea?

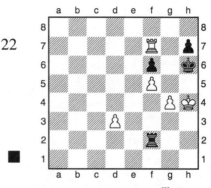

22

Does the stalemate trick **1...♖xf5** save the game?

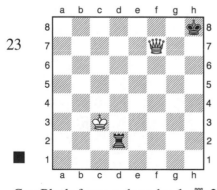

23

Can Black force a draw by **1...♖c2+** or **1...♖d3+**?

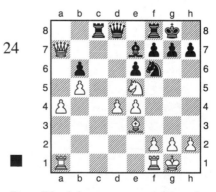

24

Does Black have a perpetual attack on the white queen by **1...♖a8 2 ♕b7 ♖b8**?

Solutions to Forcing a Draw Exercises

1) White is threatened with mate, but a rook sacrifice leads to an endless series of queen checks: **1 ♖xh7+! ♔xh7 2 ♕xg6+ ♔h8 3 ♕h6+ ♔g8 4 ♕g6+** and so on.

2) One move is enough to force the draw. After **1 ♕f2!** Black's queen is pinned and has no safe square on the diagonal between f2 and a7. Therefore the reply **1...♕xf2** is forced, but now it's stalemate.

3) Black is a pawn down and if White could extract his queen from its current awkward position he would stand to win. However, Black can take advantage of the queen's lack of mobility to force a draw: **1...♖a8** (1...♖c7? fails to 2 ♕xb6) **2 ♕b7 ♖b8 3 ♕a7 ♖a8 4 ♕b7 ♖b8** with a draw by perpetual attack on the queen.

4) White threatens ♖xh7+, but Black gets in first with **1...♖g2+!**. If White takes the rook it is stalemate, but moving his king is a draw in any case since Black has a 'rampant rook'. **2 ♔f4 ♖g4+ 3 ♔e3 ♖e4+ 4 ♔f2** (or 4 ♔d3 ♖d4+ 5 ♔c3 ♖c4+ 6 ♔b3 ♖b4+ 7 ♔a3 ♖a4+) **4...♖e2+ 5 ♔g3 ♖g2+** and there is no escape from the rook checks. This tactic is a curious combination of perpetual check and stalemate.

5) Black is a pawn down and should be happy to force a draw by perpetual attack on White's rook: **1...♘c2 2 ♖b1 ♘a3** (exploiting the pin along the b-file) **3 ♖a1 ♘c2** and the position repeats.

6) Two pawns down, White is facing defeat, and needs something special to save the game. With **1 ♖xa3!** White walks into an apparently deadly skewer but after **1...♖h3+ 2 ♔e4 ♖xa3** it is stalemate. If Black does not take the rook, then White would only be one pawn down and should save the game.

7) Black is a piece down, but can rescue the position by forcing perpetual check: **1...e3+! 2 ♔xe3 ♕g5+ 3 ♔f2** (3 ♔f3 ♕xg4+ 4 ♔e3 ♕g5+ is also a draw, but not 3 ♔d4? c5+ 4 dxc6 ♘xc6+ 5 ♔d5 ♕f6 and Black mates next move) **3...♕h4+ 4 ♔e3** (or 4 ♔g2 ♕xg4+ 5 ♔f2 ♕h4+) **4...♕g5+**, repeating the position.

8) Black's pawn cannot be stopped, so the position may appear hopeless, but White manages to draw by making good use of his king: **1 a4 ♔b4** (after 1...d4 2 a5 both sides promote, leading to a draw) **2 ♔b6!** (the key move, both supporting White's own pawn and edging nearer Black's) **2...♔xa4** (2...d4 3 a5 d3 4 a6 d2 5 a7 d1♕ 6 a8♕ is again a draw) **3 ♔c5** and White eliminates Black's pawn.

9) There are many special drawing ideas in the endgame. Here just waiting by 1 ♔h1? loses after 1...♔xh3 2 ♔g1 g4 3 ♔h1 g3 4 ♔g1 g2. Instead White changes the situation by forcing Black to take the pawn on h4 rather than h3: **1 h4! ♔xh4** (1...gxh4 2 ♔h1 is also a draw because king and rook's pawn vs king is always a draw if the defending king is in front of the pawn) **2 ♔h2!** (2 ♔g2? ♔g4 loses because Black has the *opposition*, that is to say White must move his king to one side or the other, allowing Black's king to advance) **2...♔g4 3 ♔g2 ♔f4 4 ♔f2** with the same standard draw as was mentioned in Exercise 26 on page 95; for example, **4...g4 5 ♔g2 g3 6 ♔g1 ♔f3 7 ♔f1 g2+ 8 ♔g1 ♔g3** stalemate.

10) White's queen and knight are under attack, and the obvious captures 1 ♘xd8? gxh5 and 1 ♕xe5? ♗xe6 leave Black ahead on material. To save the game White must be prepared to offer his queen: **1 ♖xf7! gxh5** (Black has no choice because after 1...♔xf7? 2

115

♘xd8+ his queen is taken with check) **2 ♖g7+ ♔h8 3 ♖h7+ ♔g8 4 ♖g7+** with perpetual check.

11) Black is threatened with ♖e8#, and passive defence by 1...♖h8? loses to 2 ♖e7 ♖f8 3 ♖b7+ ♔c8 4 ♖a7 ♔b8 5 c7+ ♔c8 6 ♖a8+, but he can save the game with a tactical trick. After **1...♖b7+!**, taking the rook is stalemate while otherwise Black drives the enemy king back and transfers his rook to an active position. This is enough to save the game; for example, **2 ♔c5 ♖b1 3 ♖e7 ♖c1+ 4 ♔d6 ♖d1+** and the check bombardment draws.

12) Black is two knights ahead, normally enough to win if there are additional pieces on the board. However, one of the paradoxes of chess is that in the absence of any other material, two knights cannot beat a lone king, so if White can exchange bishops he is safe: **1 ♗f1+ ♔b6 2 ♗c4!** (Black must avoid the bishop swap, so his reply is forced) **2...♗f5 3 ♗d3** (White continues to harass the enemy bishop) **3...♗e6 4 ♗c4** and it's a draw by repetition.

13) A piece for two pawns down, White would normally lose, but he has a hidden defence: **1 b6! axb6 2 a6 b5** (not 2...♔c8? 3 a7 ♔b7 4 d7 and White wins) **3 a7 ♗xa7** stalemate.

14) Stalemate is not the first thing that comes to mind here, especially as the h5-pawn seems free to move, which is why such ideas are often missed, even by very strong players. White can draw by giving up his rook and queen: **1 ♖a8+ ♔h7** (1...♔g7 2 ♖g8+ ♔h7 3 ♖h8+ is the same) **2 ♖h8+!♔xh8** (or 2...♔g7 3 ♖g8+) **3 ♕h6+! ♕xh6** and the h-pawn is blocked, so it is indeed stalemate.

15) White is a piece for a pawn down. This would be a guaranteed loss in most cases, but here White can draw by perpetual attack on the enemy knight: **1 ♔b6 ♘c8+ 2 ♔c7 ♘a7 3 ♔b6** (the knight cannot escape, and Black's last winning attempt is to give up the knight and make a run for the white pawns with his king) **3...♔h7 4 ♔xa7 ♔g6 5 ♔b6 ♔xf6 6 ♔c5 ♔e5 7 ♔c4** (intending ♔d3 and ♔e2) **7...♔f4** (the only chance) **8 ♔d5 ♔xf3** (8...f5 9 ♔e6 also draws) **9 ♔e5** and White wins the last black pawn.

16) White is a pawn down with his pieces under attack, so only a miracle will save him: **1 ♕xh7+!** (1 ♘f6+? ♘xf6 wins for Black) **1...♔xh7 2 ♘f6++** (double check, so the king must move) **2...♔h6** (2...♔h8?? loses to 3 ♖h3#) **3 ♖h3+ ♔g5 4 ♘h7+** (White's attack is strong enough to force a draw; indeed Black must take care not to lose) **4...♔g4** (4...♔f4?? 5 ♖h4#) **5 ♖g3+ ♔h5** (other moves lose since both 5...♔h4? 6 ♘f3+ ♔h5 7 ♖h3+ ♔g4 8 ♖h4# and 5...♔f4? 6 ♖f3+ ♔g4 7 ♗f5+ ♔h5 8 ♖h3# allow White to mate) **6 ♖h3+** with a draw by perpetual check.

17) Two pawns down, it looks hopeless for White, but there is a hidden escape route: **1 ♕b8+** (1 ♘h5? is wrong as Black plays 1...♕b1+ 2 ♔f2 ♕c2+ and only then 3...gxh5, since without a check on c7 there is no perpetual) **1...♔g7 2 ♘h5+!** (this sacrifice opens up enough lines to force perpetual check) **2...gxh5** (2...♔h6? even loses to 3 ♕f4+! g5 4 ♕f6+ ♔xh5 5 g4+ ♔h4 6 ♕h6#) **3 ♕g3+ ♔f8 4 ♕b8+** (Black cannot evade the checks) **4...♔e7 5 ♕c7+ ♔f6 6 ♕f4+ ♔g6 7 ♕g3+ ♔h6** (or 7...♔f5 8 ♕e5+ ♔g6 9 ♕g3+) **8 ♕f4+ ♔g6 9 ♕g3+** and so on.

18) This looks awkward for White since if he moves his queen, Black plays ...exd4 and is a pawn up. However, a clever defence saves White: **1 0-0!** (1 ♗xf7+? ♔xf7 2 0-0 ♕xh4 leaves Black a pawn ahead) **1...♗xc1** (1...g5 2 ♖xf4 gxf4 3 ♘f5 is slightly better for White) **2 ♗xf7+ ♔d7** (2...♔e7 3 ♘d5+ ♔d7 4 ♗e6+ ♔e8 5 ♗f7+ is also a draw, and if 2...♔f8? then

White wins by 3 ♘e6+, forking king and queen) **3 ♗e6+** and Black has no escape from the checks. For example, **3...♚e8 4 ♗f7+ ♚e7 5 ♘d5+ ♚d7 6 ♗e6+ ♚e8 7 ♗f7+**.

19) White can win after **1...♗xf7 2 gxf7 ♚xh7** by playing **3 f8♖!** with a standard rook vs king win. Not, however, 3 f8♕?, stalemating Black.

20) Black can win by transferring his king to h3: **1...♚g3! 2 ♚g1 ♚h3 3 ♚h1** (or 3 ♚f2 ♚h2 and the pawn advances) **3...g3 4 ♚g1 g2 5 ♚f2 ♚h2** and again the pawn will promote.

21) White's sacrifice doesn't work as Black has an in-between move: **1 ♘xg6? hxg6** (1...fxg6 2 ♗xg6 ♘f6! is also good) **2 ♗xg6 ♘f6!** (2...fxg6? 3 ♕xg6+ really is a draw) **3 ♕g5 fxg6** (now Black can safely take the second piece) **4 ♕xg6+ ♚h8 5 ♕h6+ ♘h7** and Black is two pieces up.

22) **1...♖xf5** is a good try, but it doesn't save the game. White continues **2 ♖xh7+! ♚xh7 3 gxf5** and wins with the extra pawn; for example, **3...♚g7 4 ♚h5 ♚h7 5 d4 ♚g7 6 d5 ♚f7 7 d6 ♚e8 8 ♚g6**, etc.

23) White can evade the checks by arranging to take the rampant rook with his queen, thereby lifting the stalemate: **1...♖c2+** (or 1...♖d3+ 2 ♚b4 ♖d4+ 3 ♚c5 and the next check can be met by a queen capture) **2 ♚b4 ♖b2+** (2...♖c4+ 3 ♕xc4) **3 ♚a3** and again there are no more useful checks, so White has a standard queen vs rook win.

24) White can evade the perpetual attack on his queen by **1...♖a8 2 ♕b7 ♖b8 3 ♕a6!** **♖a8 4 ♘c6!** (this works now that the white queen is defended by a pawn) **4...♖xa6** (4...♕c7 5 ♘xe7+ and White wins after 5...♕xe7 6 ♕xb6 or 5...♚h8 6 ♖fc1) **5 ♘xd8 ♖a8 6 ♘c6** and he keeps the two extra pawns.

Pawn Promotion

13 Test Papers

Everything you have learned so far will be put to the test in this final section. These six test papers cover all the tactical themes from earlier chapters. There is no indication which themes are important in each position – you will have to work that out for yourself. The first test is a warm-up with four positions, and the remaining tests all have six positions. The difficulty of each position is indicated by stars under the diagram, with one star being the easiest and five stars the hardest. The later tests are slightly harder than the earlier ones. You are trying to find the best move, which will generally be a win but in a few cases where you start with a bad position you need to find a draw.

It's best if you write down your answers and then compare them with the solutions (which start on page 124). There you will be awarded points according to the difficulty of the position and how well you answered. Keep a record of your scores and add them to the score-chart on page 127. Good luck!

Test Paper 1

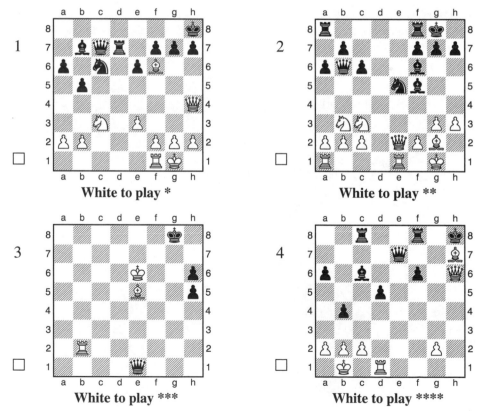

White to play *

White to play **

White to play ***

White to play ***

Test Paper 2

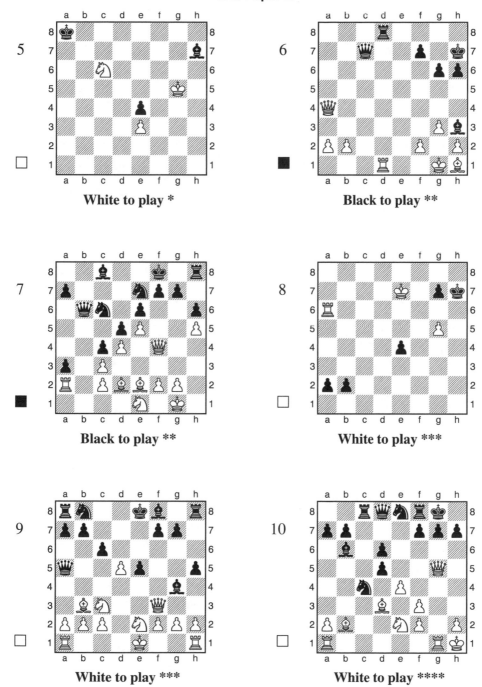

5 White to play *

6 Black to play **

7 Black to play **

8 White to play ***

9 White to play ***

10 White to play ****

119

Test Paper 3

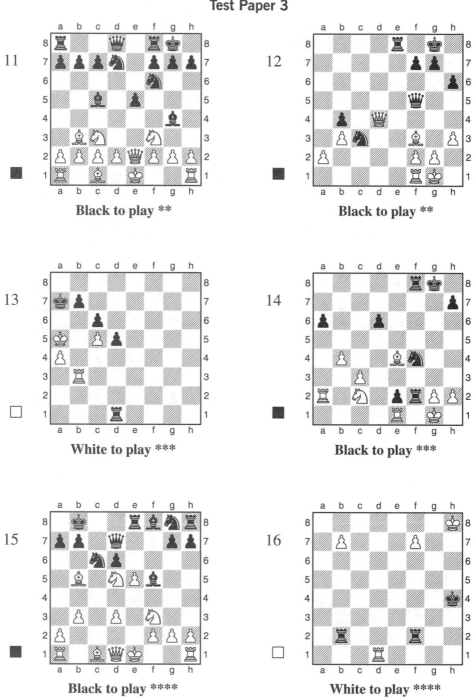

11 Black to play **

12 Black to play **

13 White to play ***

14 Black to play ***

15 Black to play ****

16 White to play ****

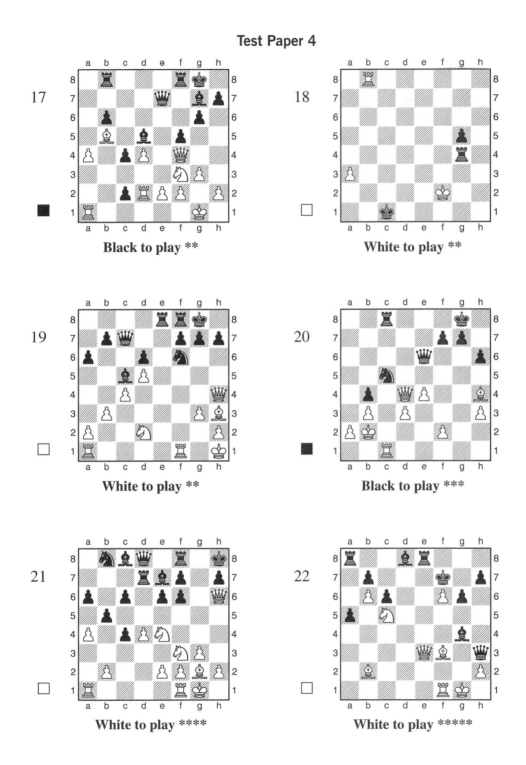

17   **Black to play ****

18   **White to play ****

19   **White to play ****

20   **Black to play *****

21   **White to play ******

22   **White to play *******

23 Black to play **

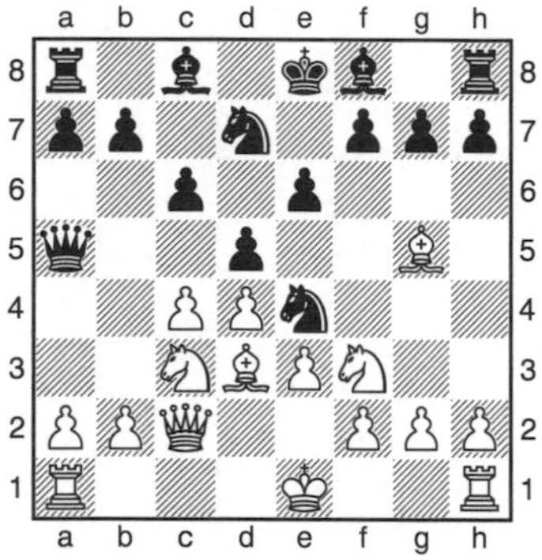

24 White to play **

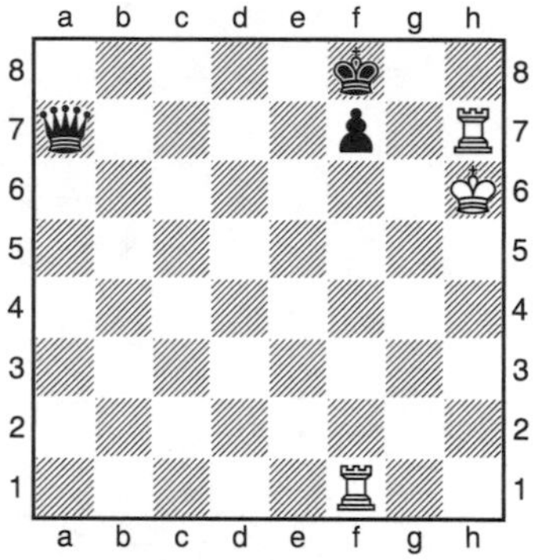

25 White to play **

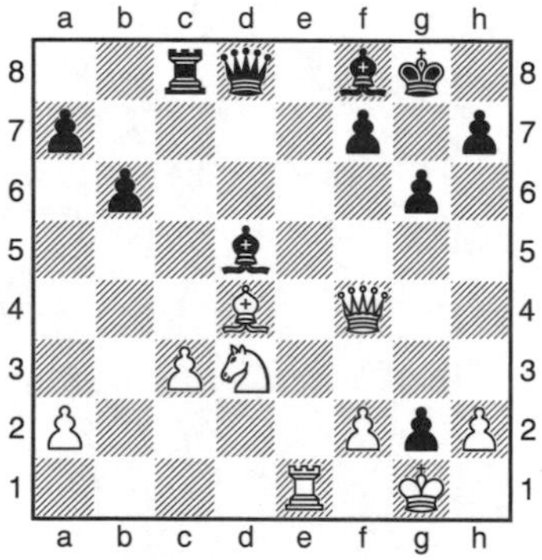

26 White to play ***

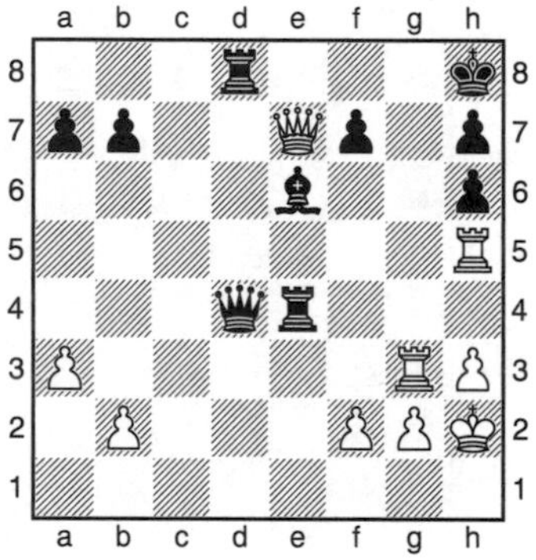

27 White to play ****

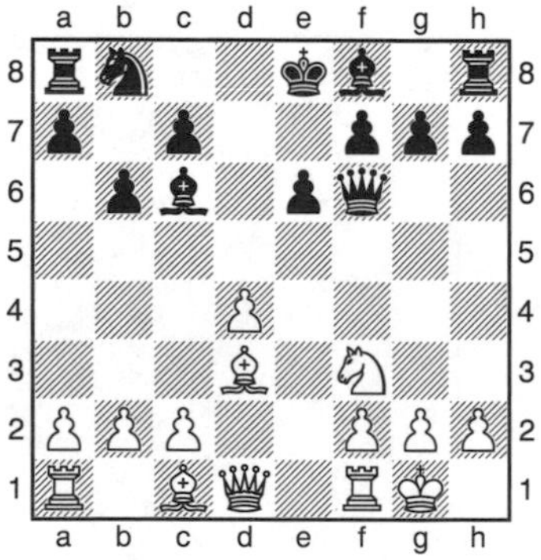

28 Black to play *****

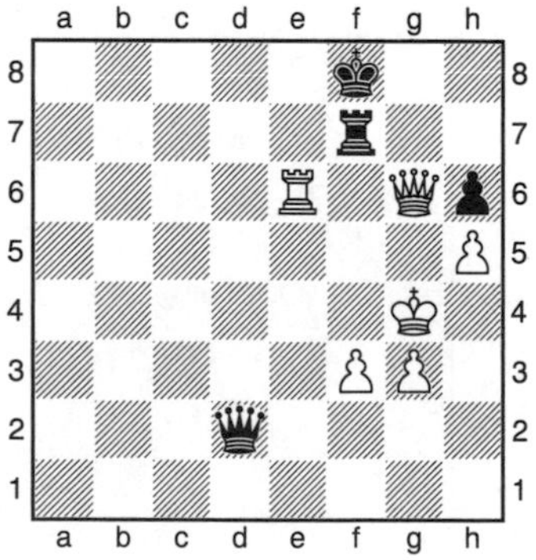

Test Paper 6

29

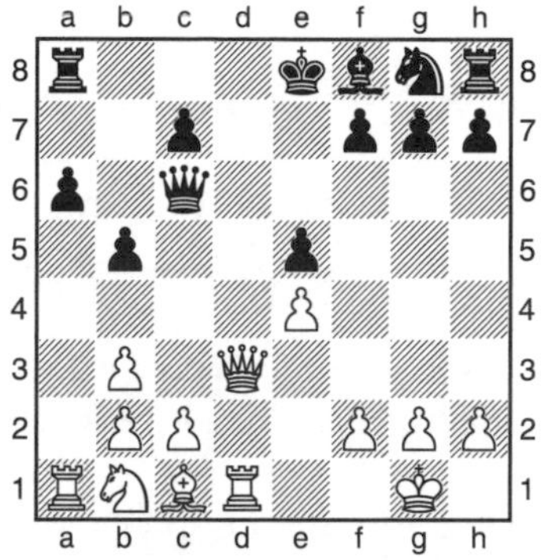

White to play **

30

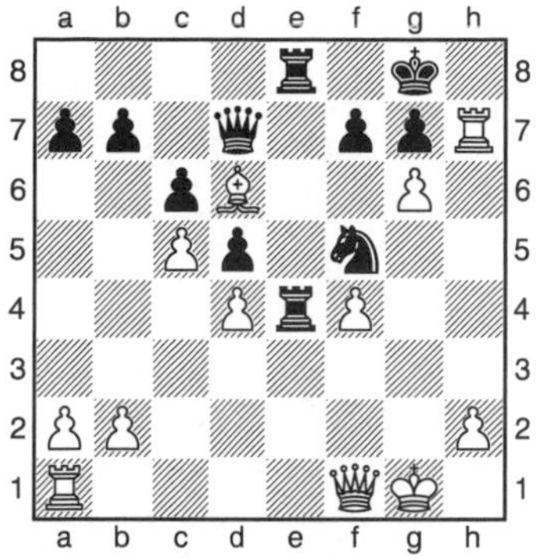

White to play ***

31

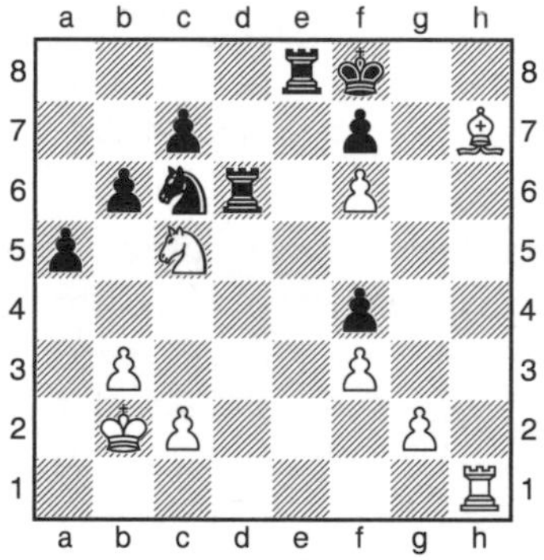

White to play ***

32

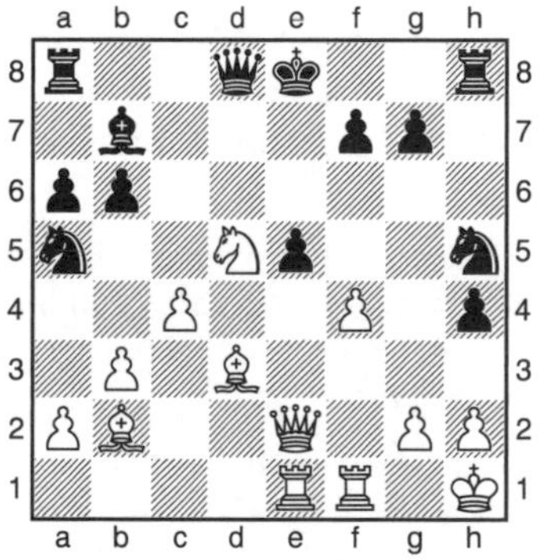

Black to play ****

33

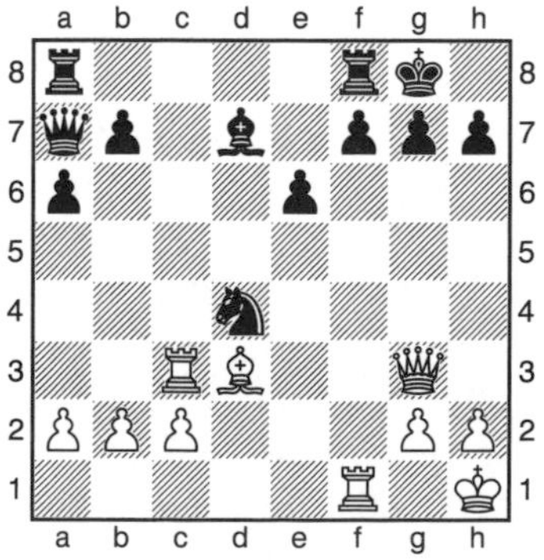

White to play ****

34

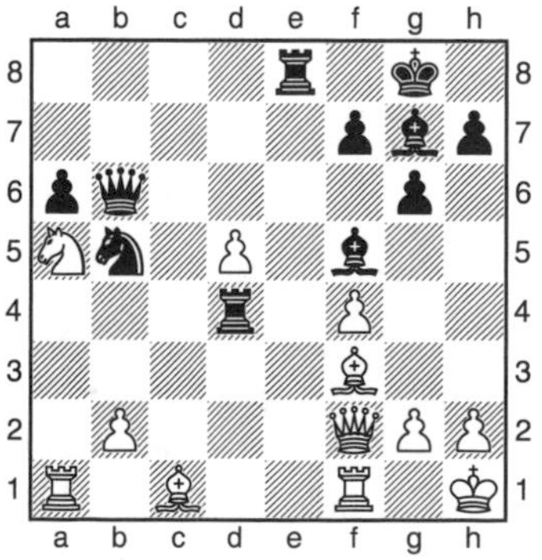

Black to play *****

Solutions to Test Papers

Test Paper 1

1) White can force mate by **1 ♕h6!**, using the pin of the g7-pawn. There's nothing better than **1...gxf6**, but then **2 ♕f8#**. (1 point)

2) The g-pawn can advance and drive away the f6-bishop, which is guarding Black's knight: **1 g4!** (gaining time by attacking the bishop on f5) **1...♗g6 2 g5** and White wins a piece. (2 points)

3) White has to chase the enemy king into position before administering the final blow: **1 ♖b8+! ♔h7 2 ♖h8+ ♔g6 3 ♖g8+ ♔h7 4 ♖g7+ ♔h8** and now everything is ready for the discovered check **5 ♖g1+**, winning the queen. (3 points)

4) Here White has a choice of discovered checks, but only one leads to victory: **1 ♗f5+! ♔g8 2 ♗e6+! ♕xe6** (2...♖f7 and 2...♕f7 are both answered by 3 ♖h1 followed by ♕h8#) **3 ♕g6+ ♔h8 4 ♖h1+** and mate next move. (4 points)

Test Paper 2

5) White first confines the bishop and then wins it: **1 ♘e7! ♔b7 2 ♔h6**. (1 point)

6) There's a potential mate by ...♖xd1#, but first the white queen must be deflected. **1...♕c4!** does the trick as Black either wins the queen or gives mate after **2 ♕xc4 ♖xd1+ 3 ♕f1 ♖xf1#**. (2 points)

7) The a3-pawn is attacked and appears to be blockaded, but a single move changes the picture: **1...♕b2! 2 ♖xb2 axb2** and the pawn promotes, leaving White a rook down. (2 points)

8) Black's far-advanced pawns are scary, but White's lone pawn wins the game all by itself: **1 ♔f7! a1♕** (1...b1♕ is the same) **2 ♖h6+! gxh6 3 g6+ ♔h8 4 g7+ ♔h7 5 g8♕#**. (3 points)

9) White wins with a surprising and unusual combination: **1 ♕xf7+!! ♔xf7 2 dxc6+ ♔g6** (other moves are similar; for example, 2...♗e6 3 cxb7 ♗xb3 4 cxb3) **3 cxb7** and Black cannot prevent bxa8♕, which will leave White a rook ahead. (3 points)

10) This is a classic mating combination from the 19th century, and similar ideas are still claiming victims today: **1 ♕xg7+! ♘xg7 2 ♖xg7+ ♔h8 3 ♖g8++!** (the key move; it's double check so Black must take the rook) **3...♔xg8 4 ♖g1+ ♕g5 5 ♖xg5#**. (4 points)

Test Paper 3

11) The f3-knight is pinned and cannot move after **1...e4!**. White has little choice but to take the pawn, and then **2 ♘xe4 ♘xe4 3 ♕xe4 ♖e8** is a deadly second pin, costing White his queen. (2 points)

12) The bishop is the only thing preventing a knight fork on e2, so Black just eliminates it: **1...♕xf3! 2 gxf3 ♘e2+** and Black wins a piece. (2 points)

13) White is a pawn down with weak, isolated pawns, and could well lose if he does not take advantage of the momentary chance to save the game using stalemate: **1 ♖b1! ♖d2 2 ♖b2 ♖d3 3 ♖b3** (White continues the face-off between the rooks) **3...♖d4** (the only way to avoid the unwelcome attentions of the white rook, but now it's a different stalemate) **4 ♖xb7+! ♔xb7** stalemate. (2 points for finding 1 ♖b1! and 1 additional point if you saw the sacrifice on b7)

14) Black forces mate by a neat promotion tactic: **1...Rf1+! 2 Rxf1 Nh3+ 3 gxh3 exf1W#.** (3 points)

15) A spectacular queen sacrifice sets up a double check leading to mate: **1...Nxe5!!** (attacking the undefended b5-bishop) **2 Bxd7** (otherwise White loses a piece) **2...Nxf3++ 3 Kf1 Bxd3+! 4 Wxd3** (or 4 We2 Bxe2#) **4...Re1#.** (4 points)

16) This position shows an entertaining double deflection. The black rooks are holding back the white pawns, but White can play a rather weird deflection-plus-fork combination: **1 Rd2!! Rbxd2** (1...Rxf7 2 Rxb2, 1...Rxb7 2 Rxf2 and 1...Rfxd2 2 f8W Rxb7 3 Wf4+ all win for White) **2 b8W Rxf7** (if Black does not take, the other pawn will also promote) **3 Wb4+** followed by **4 Wxd2**, with the winning material advantage of queen vs rook. (3 points for finding 1 Rd2!! and 1 extra point if you saw the whole line up to 3 Wb4+)

Test Paper 4

17) **1...Wa3!** both attacks the a1-rook and threatens to promote. White might as well take the queen, but after **2 Rxa3 c1W+ 3 Kg2 Wxa3** Black has won a rook. (2 points)

18) The position would be a draw, except for **1 Rb4! Rxb4** (Black's rook is effectively trapped and he cannot avoid a rook swap) **2 axb4** and the b-pawn will promote. (2 points)

19) A knight on f6 is often a good defender of Black's kingside. Here White eliminates it to launch a mating attack: **1 Rxf6! gxf6 2 Bf5** followed by mate with **Wxh7#.** (2 points)

20) The white queen must defend d3, allowing Black a stunning tactic: **1...We5!** and now **2 Wxe5 Nxd3+ 3 Kb1 Rxc1#** is mate, while 2 Rc4 also loses after **2...Nxd3+ 3 Kc2** (or 3 Kb1 Wxd4 4 Rxd4 Rc1#) **3...Wxd4**, winning the white queen. (3 points)

21) White wins with a tricky double knight sacrifice: **1 Nfg5!!** (this is solely to clear the way for the bishop to reach e4) **1...fxg5 2 Nf6!** (now White decoys the e7-bishop to f6, so that Be4 cannot be met by ...f5) **2...Bxf6 3 Be4** with mate next move by **4 Wxh7#.** (4 points)

22) White wins with a cascade of sacrifices: **1 Bd5+!** (clearing the f-file because the rook will need to defend the pawn when it advances to f7) **1...cxd5** (1...Kf8 2 Wxe8+ is similar) **2 Wxe8+! Rxe8 3 f7+ Kf8** (3...Re7 4 f8W#) **4 Bg7+!** (the important final point) **4...Kxg7 5 f8W#.** (5 points, but only if you have seen the whole line up to 4 Bg7+!)

Test Paper 5

23) Similar to Exercise 4 on page 47, here's another example of the 'stray piece on g5 drops off' theme: **1...Nxg5! 2 Nxg5** (the undefended g5-knight is now a target for a discovered attack) **2...dxc4** attacks both the knight and the d3-bishop, and so wins a piece. (2 points)

24) White wins with a skewer: **1 Rh8+!** (1 Rhxf7+? Wxf7 2 Rxf7+ Kxf7 is only a draw) **1...Ke7 2 Rxf7+! Kxf7 3 Rh7+** and Black's queen falls. (2 points)

25) White can exploit the weak d4-h8 diagonal by a preliminary deflection which draws the black queen away from its control of f6: **1 Re8! Wxe8** (Black may as well take since there is no way to both cover f6 and save the rook on c8) **2 Wf6** and White will mate on h8 or g7. (2 points)

26) White wins with an amazing tactic: **1 Rd5!!** (this spectacular move allows the rook to be taken by three different pieces, but each one leads to disaster for Black) **1...Bxd5** (the other lines are 1...♖xd5 2 ♕f8# and 1...♕xd5 2 ♕f6#) **2 ♕xd8+** and mate next move. (3 points)

27) There's an unexpected twist to this tactic: **1 ♗g5! ♗xf3** (this looks like an escape clause, but White closes the net around the black queen in any case) **2 ♕d2! ♕xd4** (the only square for the queen, but now it falls to a discovered attack) **3 ♗b5+** followed by **4 ♕xd4**. (2 points for finding 1 ♗g5! and 2 more if you saw both 1...♗xf3 and the reply 2 ♕d2!).

28) Black forces a draw in which both his rook and his queen are 'rampant': **1...♖f4+!** (1...♕f4+? 2 gxf4 ♖xf4+ doesn't work as White can win by 3 ♔g3 ♖xf3+ 4 ♔h4 ♖h3+ 5 ♔g4 ♖g3+ 6 ♔f5 ♖f3+ 7 ♔e5 ♖e3+ 8 ♕e4) **2 ♔h3** (2 gxf4 ♕xf4+ 3 ♔h3 ♕h2+ 4 ♔g4 ♕f4+ is similar) **2...♖h4+!** **3 ♔xh4** (or 3 gxh4 ♕h2+ 4 ♔g4 ♕f4+) **3...♕h2+ 4 ♔g4 ♕xg3+** (4...♕h4+ is equally good and also earns full marks) **5 ♔f5 ♕f4+ 6 ♔xf4** stalemate. (5 points if you saw up to Black's 4th move)

Test Paper 6

29) White has an instant win with the double deflection **1 ♖xa6!**. This pulls one of the black pieces away from defending d7 or d8 and wins after **1...♕xa6 2 ♕d7#** or **1...♖xa6 2 ♕d8#**. (2 points)

30) Black's king is in danger, and by decoying it to h8 White can bring in his queen with gain of time: **1 ♖h8+! ♔xh8 2 ♕h3+ ♘h6** (or 2...♔g8 3 ♕h7#) **3 ♕xd7** and White wins queen for rook. (3 points)

31) Black's king is trapped on the back rank, but he threatens to take the f6-pawn and so release the king. White can prevent this by first deflecting the rook on d6: **1 ♘d7+!** (there is also a decoy element here, as the rook is exposed to attack on d7) **1...♖xd7 2 ♗f5!** (attacking d7 and threatening ♖h8#; after 2 ♗e4 ♔g8, 3 ♗xc6? ♖dd8 4 ♗xe8 ♖xe8 is only equal, so White should repeat the position by 3 ♗h7+) **2...♔g8** (2...♘e7 3 ♖h8+ ♘g8 4 ♗h7 mates next move) **3 ♗xd7** (unluckily for Black, he now finds two pieces forked by the white bishop) **3...♖e6 4 ♗xe6** with a decisive material advantage for White. (2 points for 1 ♘d7+! and 1 further point if you saw up to 3 ♗xd7)

32) Black's h8-rook stands opposite the white king on h1 and by blasting the three intervening pieces out of the way Black can open the h-file and launch a mating attack: **1...♘g3+!** **2 hxg3 hxg3+ 3 ♔g1** (now a final sacrifice allows Black to transfer his queen to the h-file with gain of time) **3...♖h1+! 4 ♔xh1 ♕h4+ 5 ♔g1 ♕h2#**. (4 points, but only if you saw the whole line up to mate)

33) A piece down, White must scramble to force a draw: **1 ♗xh7+! ♔xh7 2 ♕xg7+!** (an amazing double sacrifice clears the way for perpetual check by the rook) **2...♔xg7 3 ♖g3+ ♔h6 4 ♖h3+ ♔g5 5 ♖g3+ ♔h4** and Black cannot escape from the checks. (4 points if you saw White's first two moves)

34) **1...♖d1!** (a surprising move based on the discovered attack against the white queen) **2 ♕xb6** (there is nothing better, since 2 ♗xd1 ♕xf2 3 ♖xf2 ♖e1+ mates) **2...♖xf1+ 3 ♔g1 ♖ee1** (you also earn full marks for the alternative win 3...♖xg1+ 4 ♔xg1 ♗d4+ 5 ♔f1 ♗d3+) **4 ♗e3** (4 ♕xf1 ♖xf1#) **4...♖xg1+ 5 ♗xg1 ♖xa1** and Black has won a rook. (3 points for 1...♖d1!, and 2 more for seeing up to Black's third move).

Score-Table

Test number	Maximum score	Your score
1	10	
2	15	
3	18	
4	18	
5	18	
6	21	
Total	100	

Rate your score:

0-20	Revision necessary!
21-40	Focus on your weaker areas
41-60	Shows potential
61-80	Promising talent
81-90	Potential international player
91-95	Potential Master strength
96-100	Potential Grandmaster

Further Reading

If you enjoy solving positions for yourself, you might like the following books:

Chess Puzzles for Kids (Gambit, 2012): Contains 100 tactical ideas and some test papers. It is at a similar level to the current book.

Learn Chess Tactics (Gambit, 2004): Deals with similar tactical themes to the current book, but at a higher level.

1001 Deadly Checkmates (Gambit, 2011): Covers exclusively tactics leading to mate. The level is similar to the current book, although there a few more difficult exercises.

Other related titles:

Chess Tactics for Kids (Gambit, 2003): This focuses on 50 important tactical ideas, some of which are featured in the current book.

How to Beat Your Dad at Chess (Gambit, 1998): At a slightly lower level than the current book, this covers 50 common mating patterns.

PIN

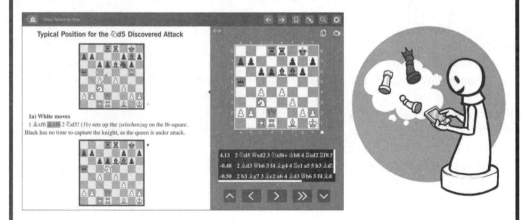